Aimee Byrd, in *The Sexual Reformatio*  for nothing less than a reformation and discusses sexuality that more f vision. Byrd powerfully calls us to dis embodiment as male and female resonates with the great marriage of heaven and earth made possible through the incarnation and the marriage supper of the lamb.

—**Timothy C. Tennent,** president,
Asbury Theological Seminary

This is a book that will grow your soul. In the midst of albeit important debates about the meaning of masculinity, femininity, authority, and submission, Aimee invites us to rise above and listen—listen to Jesus singing over us, pointing us to redemptive sexuality centered on himself. Instead of viewing each other as rivals for power, let's join in the song—the Song of Songs—and embrace each other as gifts. May that song of the sexual reformation lead to our dance of celebration!

—**Sheila Wray Gregoire,** author of *The Great Sex Rescue*

¡Viva la reformación! Aimee Byrd calls us back to Scripture, and to the Song of Songs specifically, as a way of reorienting our fallen views of personhood, sexuality, and Christ's love for his bride. The book is a rich exercise in the Christian imagination, birthed by Scripture, rooted in tradition, and enkindled by the Holy Spirit. Take up and sing!

—**Joshua M. McNall,** associate professor of pastoral
theology, Oklahoma Wesleyan University

Beyond revolution, we need a reformation, and Byrd perfectly explains why as she implores readers to question hierarchal roles baked into evangelicalism. Through the oft-overlooked book of Song of Songs, she beckons the church to consider a richer, more robust understanding of the sexes and honor the inherent dignity and embodied personhood of men and women. Her insights will untangle your beliefs about sexuality and reform them for the flourishing of all.

—**Tiffany Bluhm,** author of *Prey Tell: Why We Silence
Women Who Tell the Truth and How Everyone Can Speak Up*

This isn't your grandfather's talk on sex and gender in the Bible! Aimee Byrd delivers what every Christian needs to consider: the rich tapestry of sexuality interlaced throughout Scripture via the Song of Songs! Byrd's commitment to Scripture as the primary voice on sex liberates her to make unique insights not merely reactive to gender discussions that we've become so used to. Sex (in every sense of the word) matters, but in ways we've often failed to consider. Byrd offers us an easy-to-read and biblically honed theological foray through which we can check ourselves lest we continue to wreck ourselves. Consequently, Scripture's world of thinking springs to life, and our currently muddled conversations about sex clarify.

—**Dru Johnson,** associate professor of biblical studies, director of the Center for Hebraic Thought

Byrd contends that we are in need of a more robust theology of sexuality —what does it mean to be man? Woman? Humans in relationship with one another? So much that is written in this category is combative, overly simplistic, or individualistic. Byrd turns to Scripture, specifically the Song of Songs, to ponder these matters anew. She finds there a love canticle that showcases the beauty of unity, individual uniqueness and gifting, and desire at its best. Throughout, Byrd points to the example of the love of God made flesh in Jesus Christ. This book is a great starting place to move beyond old battles stuck in stalemate or tired of fighting.

—**Nijay K. Gupta,** professor of New Testament, Northern Seminary

Where liberal scholarship diminishes Christ in the Song of Songs, Aimee Byrd exalts him according to classical exegesis. In conversation with great expositors from Nyssa and Augustine to Spurgeon and Jenson, Byrd challenges captive cultural interpretations, perverse gender discussions, and fallen power dynamics between men and women. Such profound biblical insights demonstrate why the Bride must again honor the lay prophets God empowers with his Spirit to turn our desire toward the Bridegroom's glory.

—**Malcolm B. Yarnell,** author of *Royal Priesthood in the English Reformation, God the Trinity: Biblical Portraits,* and *Who Is the Holy Spirit?*

THE
SEXUAL
REFORMATION

RESTORING THE DIGNITY
AND PERSONHOOD
OF MAN AND WOMAN

AIMEE BYRD

ZONDERVAN
REFLECTIVE

ZONDERVAN REFLECTIVE

The Sexual Reformation
Copyright © 2022 by Aimee Byrd

Requests for information should be addressed to:
Zondervan, *3900 Sparks Dr. SE, Grand Rapids, Michigan 49546*

Zondervan titles may be purchased in bulk for educational, business, fundraising, or sales promotional use. For information, please email SpecialMarkets@Zondervan.com.

ISBN 978-0-310-12566-2 (audio)

Library of Congress Cataloging-in-Publication Data

Names: Byrd, Aimee, 1975- author.
Title: The sexual reformation : restoring the dignity and personhood of man and woman / Aimee
    Byrd.
Description: Grand Rapids : Zondervan, 2022.
Identifiers: LCCN 2021034807 (print) | LCCN 2021034808 (ebook) | ISBN 9780310125648
    (paperback) | ISBN 9780310125655 (ebook)
Subjects: LCSH: Bible. Song of Solomon--Criticism, interpretation, etc. | Sex role--Biblical teaching.
Classification: LCC BS1485.6.S45 B97 2022 (print) | LCC BS1485.6.S45 (ebook) | DDC 261.8/357
    --dc23/eng/20211118
LC record available at https://lccn.loc.gov/2021034807
LC ebook record available at https://lccn.loc.gov/2021034808

I dedicate this book to my dear friend Anna Anderson, whom I've spent hours and hours with hiking and discussing the wondrous typology unfolded herein. Anna, I don't know where my thoughts end and yours begin in these pages, as your fingerprints are all over them. You are a special gift from the Lord.

CONTENTS

ACKNOWLEDGMENTS

This is a different kind of book than I've written before, even as it builds off the rest. And if I am being upfront, it was conceived in the midst of a lot of pain. But now I am at a place where I can acknowledge how rejection, neglect, betrayal, and even spiritual abuse drove me to seek the presence of Christ. I am thankful for the trials because of the riches they led me to. They also brought clarity, which led to the title and handle of the book.

I want to thank some important friends who have influenced my thinking and helped me as my work developed. You will notice me citing my friend Anna Anderson throughout the book. God has brought our lives together in the most interesting ways. As a result, her work as an academic has intersected with my own writing projects. We've shared many moments in awe together over the wonder of the triune God and his love for us. I chuckle when I think of how we must have looked to any outsiders passing by on our "theology hikes," while we were enthralled in conversation, passionately and unapologetically talking a mile a minute. As I said in my dedication to her, I don't know where my thoughts begin and hers end. I'm sure that after seeing her footnoted throughout, you will wish you were part of our "personal communications" and look forward to future publishing from her. I'm thankful for her academic contributions, sending much good research my way, and reading over most of my chapters. Heck, I'm even thankful for her emails because they are full of brilliant insight. More so, I am incredibly thankful for her friendship—I learn from her in so many ways, and I enjoy every minute.

I also want to thank Rachel Miller and Valerie Hobbs for their friendship, support, and theological conversation. My friendship with them has been formative in my quest to restore the dignity and personhood of men and women. Again, these are fellow laborers in sexual reformation for the church. For that, we've been through some suffering together, but we've grown closer to the One who is "notable among ten thousand" (Song 5:10).

Working with Zondervan again is an honor. I'm grateful for the investment Katya Covrett has made in me as an author in developing the handle for the book and editing, but also in time spent getting to know me and for offering research suggestions, sharpening conversation, and providing care. The whole team at Zondervan is a delight to work with and just to get to know as people.

And I'm thankful for my husband, Matt, who seems to know intuitively what subjects I continue to dig into books for. His gift of love indeed models that of the true Bridegroom in that he is the first to love, the first to give, and the first to sacrifice.

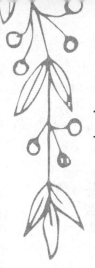

Intro

REFORMATION LOOKS FORWARD

Imagine there is a heaven.

In 1971 John Lennon released what became his bestselling single as a solo artist, "Imagine." He asked us to imagine a world with no heaven, no borders, and no possessions. This imagining was supposed to help promote peace, as we live only for today and no longer have reasons for war, greed, or hunger. If we could just get rid of the realities of God, land, and our basic needs, we could come together as one. We would love each other.

John Lennon was wrong about that. We aren't God, and we wouldn't exist without him. But imagining that we could, we would have no goodness, as all goodness comes from him. The problem is not the gifts he's given us but the corruption of our own hearts. The solution for peace isn't imagining no heaven; the solution is setting our eyes on the beautiful truth. The solution is to have an eschatological imagination,[1] to think deeply about our ultimate aim.

Imagine heaven and earth coming together—a new heaven and new earth. Imagine a triune God who created us to have eternal communion with him and with one another

---

1. Trevor Hart, "Eschatological Imagination," *Transpositions: Theology, Imagination and the Arts* (blog), April 29, 2011, http://www.transpositions.co.uk/eschatological-imagination/. *Eschatological* refers to humanity's final destination.

there. Imagine that this God created us as icons, or representative symbols, of himself, showcasing a great love story—the story of the outgoing, overflowing love of the triune God. Maybe it is hard to imagine this kind of love. But give it a try. Imagine that we are created to share covenantally in the Father's love for the Son, in the Holy Spirit. Imagine that our very bodies tell the story of a gift given in eternity—a gift of a bride to the Son. Imagine man and woman revealing the deep mystery of an eternal trinitarian covenant that is prefigured in creation.

The triune God loves us. Imagine that.

He made man from the soil of the land that he gave him. And he breathed life into him. He made the heavens as a testimony to the glory of his dwelling place, to which we are called. He made woman from man, her very presence beckoning him to the ultimate hope—or telos—of mankind as the collective bride of Christ. Created second, she represents the second order—the final act of creation—arrayed with the glory and radiance of the Son (Rev. 21:11). In this way, she is the glory of the man (1 Cor. 11:7). Man was to pass through probation, with his bride, to ascend to the holy mountain, Zion, which her very body represents.[2] She, as his necessary ally and partner, was to be a corresponding strength in their mission to receive the great reward of eternal communion with God for them and their progeny.

Our imaginations are depraved because our whole selves are depraved from the fall. Adam, as federal representative of mankind, failed to obtain our final sabbath. But Jesus Christ, the second Adam, left his Father and mother-Zion glory-realm

---

2. See Aimee Byrd, "Women, Wells, and Weddings," *The Mod* (blog), Modern Reformation, October 7, 2019, https://www.whitehorseinn.org/2019/10/the-mod-women-wells-and-weddings/.

to cleave to his bride (Gen. 2:24) and ascend with her to the holy of holies.[3] Our bodies speak this good news.

You see, John Lennon was right in one sense. Things are not as they should be. And what we imagine makes a difference in how we find peace for ourselves and one another. But thankfully our imagination does not have to be baseless, wishful thinking. That would get us nowhere. Our God gives us the metanarrative—the overarching story that gives meaning to all other stories—to root it in. He communicates with us through his living Word, gives us sacraments to ratify his Word, as well as symbols that remind us of it over and over. Imagination comes alive in understanding truth.

Maybe you think my imagination has gone a bit off track. There's a lot to fill in here. That's what I do in this book. I am evoking a sexual reformation in my title. My first chapter makes the case that the church needs this reformation. But first I set the melody. While reformation requires polemics, more importantly it is based on the eschatological vision God reveals to us in his living Word. As Bill Dennison notes about J. Gresham Machen's theological method, any crisis we address "calls not for confrontation and restoration of the visible culture; rather, it calls for a true knowledge and understanding of the person of God and the 'unseen world,' the kingdom of heaven."[4] The church continuously needs to look back to retrieve what the saints have historically confessed, while reforming her teachings according to the Scriptures. All of this is done to move the church forward. Her eyes are not fixed on the past but on the

---

3. See Anna Anderson, "Van Til's Representational Principal Applied to the Woman," Academia, December 16, 2020, 19, https://www.academia.edu/44870840/VAN_TIL_S_REPRESENTATIONAL_PRINCIPLE_APPLIED_TO_THE_WOMAN.

4. Bill Dennison, "J. Gresham Machen's Theological Method," appendix to J. Gresham Machen, *Things Unseen: A Systematic Introduction to the Christian Faith and Reformed Theology* (Glenside, PA: Westminster Seminary Press, 2020), 428, digital download, https://wm.wts.edu/content/dennison-article-2.

person of Jesus Christ who is ushering her behind the veil into his inner chambers. Reformation moves forward.

There's a whole book in the Bible that exercises our imaginations with this metanarrative of which I speak, or shall I say, sing. Yes, this book is even a song—the Song of all songs. It brings us into the unseen world that is to come. With the Song of Songs guiding us, we will explore the theological meaning behind our sexes, helping Christians to better understand our sexuality as a gift and to grasp the eschatological story our bodies tell of Christ's love for his church. As the Holy Spirit is speaking to the churches through his living Word today, we see that he is beckoning her.

I am humbled to enter into this Song. In one sense, I feel like a small child dressing up in her mother's wedding gown. But my Bridegroom, Jesus Christ, has adorned me with it. Each time I enter in, or put on the gown, I see that I have grown just a little more into it. I'm only beginning to discover the different jewels embroidered into its fabric—the discovery of one uncovers many dazzling others inviting inspection. I can hardly believe it's for me. Nevertheless, it provokes me to beckon many others to its beauty. Some may think I look foolish, that I am in over my head to try it on. I am happy to have the help of the many in the church who have gone before me. I am thankful for them, for we need one another to point out all the glorious jewels.

But how can I talk about the Song in one metaphor when it is full of mixed metaphors? Does that not show us that sometimes one metaphor does not suffice to point us to what awaits Christ's bride? One just cannot contain the rich meaning that is bursting forth! The Song of Songs is also like the first miracle Jesus performed, which fittingly was at a wedding. We've been dreaming about this wedding, celebrating and making our hearts glad with wine. When we drink up all the wine, what does Jesus do? He turns the water of our understanding into new wine. The good news explodes in the Song. It is the best wine that we didn't know we were missing—intimacy with our Bridegroom. It is the wine that we are invited to intoxicate ourselves with.

My soul has been deeply ministered to in studying the Song of Songs. Whether you agree with me or not on all my interpretive points, I am confident that God's words to his church in the Song of Songs will bless you. I speak from the perspective of one trying to grow into the dress. But I trust my Savior is getting me ready for that great day. One of the gems I found is the recovery of the dignity and personhood of both man and woman that is enfleshed in its lyrics, and as we will see, unfolds throughout the metanarrative of Scripture. What I mean by *enfleshed* is that it is so real that we wear it; it is given bodily form and expression. I am honored to have the opportunity to write about this. And yet there is so much more. I do hope that the biggest takeaway for the reader is the awe of beholding our God.

But before we can sip the wine, I need to present the need for sexual reformation in the church. Like I said, reformation requires polemics. When we look forward eschatologically —to our future glorification and the consummation of all things—we see more clearly the need for reform. And we have to name the maladies for which God's Word shows the remedies. My first chapter surveys the messages we are receiving in the church about what it means to be a man or a woman. Then I will introduce the Song that is given to the church to sing. I interact with numerous commentators and preachers on the Song, old and new. The reader will notice that I engage with some Roman Catholic writings on the Song and on the meaningfulness of our sexes. This is not because I am moving away from my confessional Protestant convictions, but rather because I am cognizant of the heritage that we share as the church universal and am happy to retrieve rich teaching from our shared confessional roots.

I also should alert the reader to the sensuous nature of the Song. I do not shy away from the language of sexual imagery used to teach us about the spousal love of God. I hope the reader will concur that it is tastefully done and is not reductive.

With these matters taken care of, we will begin to swish the wine in our mouths and look at some of the nuptial jewels[5] and how they propel us forward to our telos. We will find peace. Imagine that.

---

5. I just mixed those metaphors nice and well.

Chapter One

DO WE REALLY NEED A REFORMATION?

Let's just admit it. Even the church is still confused about what it means to be a man or a woman. Sure, a plethora of Christian books instructing Christians on this matter are available—more than ever. There's even a parachurch organization that has been thriving for more than thirty years with its own confessional statements on "biblical manhood and womanhood," providing articles, journals, books, teaching resources, and conferences.[1] While secular society is talking about sexuality in terms of liberation, this movement in the church defines manhood and womanhood in terms of roles. And so this is what many in the evangelical church, through the resources of this parachurch organization, have been teaching about our sexual distinction:

> At the heart of mature masculinity is a sense of benevolent responsibility to lead, provide for and protect women in ways appropriate to a man's differing relationships.
>
> At the heart of mature femininity is a freeing disposition to affirm, receive, and nurture strength and leadership

---

1. The Council on Biblical Manhood and Womanhood was founded in 1987.

from worthy men in ways appropriate to a woman's differing relationships.[2]

According to these definitions, what it means to be a man is potency in benevolent action toward women—they lead, provide, and protect women. And what it means to be a woman is, well, affirming this male potency—they affirm, receive, and nurture worthy men. What is woman's contribution? Where is any reciprocal enrichment in this? How do these definitions account for the personhood of men and women as "unique and unrepeatable" human beings?[3] Moreover, where is Christ in these definitions? They are merely horizontal.

The Council on Biblical Manhood and Womanhood (CBMW), which provided these definitions, also composed an official statement to affirm the distinction between manhood and womanhood. It is called the Danvers Statement.[4] This came at a pivotal time when Christians wanted to respond to the messages of sexual promiscuity and gender fluidity in our surrounding secular culture. Notice how the affirmations in the Danvers Statement center male/female distinction in roles:

1. Both Adam and Eve were created in God's image, equal before God as persons and distinct in their manhood and womanhood (Gen. 1:26–27; 2:18).
2. Distinctions in masculine and feminine roles are ordained by God as part of the created order, and

---

2. John Piper, "A Vision of Biblical Complementarity," in *Recovering Biblical Manhood and Womanhood*, ed. John Piper and Wayne Grudem (1991; repr., Wheaton, IL: Crossway, 2006), 35–36 (capitalized in the original).

3. See John Paul II, *Man and Woman He Created Them: A Theology of the Body*, trans. Michael Waldstein (Boston: Pauline Books & Media, 1986, 2006), TOB 15:4, 188.

4. The Danvers Statement, Council on Biblical Manhood and Womanhood, https://cbmw.org/about/danvers-statement/.

should find an echo in every human heart (Gen. 2:18, 21–24; 1 Cor. 11:7–9; 1 Tim. 2:12–14).[5]

As it turns out from the following affirmations in the Danvers Statement, these roles are defined as male headship—which is synonymous with male authority—and female submission.[6] Our "roles," specifically what we have agency to do or not do, encapsulate our God-given sexual distinction. And somehow the word *role*, which is not even found in most English translations of Scripture and which arose from the theater, meaning "to play a part," is now being used as an ontological, fixed marker of our sexuality.[7] I use the word *ontological* because now CBMW is speaking to the nature of who we are. This subtle shift of the meaning of *role* speaks to the very essence of what it means to be a man or a woman. As their president put it, "CBMW exists to promote the Danvers vision."[8] And so its promotion leads to teaching that men both initiate and have the final say.[9] The woman is warned not to do "typically masculine things" like strength training, or else her feminine needs may not be met.[10] The man takes charge in cultural settings, such as ordering at a restaurant, driving the car, and being the first to extend his hand in greeting. He also needs to be careful how he holds a woman's purse.[11] According to what we've seen in

---

5. Danvers Statement.

6. See Danvers Statement, particularly affirmations 3–6.

7. See Kevin Giles, *What the Bible Really Says about Women* (Eugene, OR: Cascade Books, 2018), 13–14. "It is important to note that the word 'role' is rarely found in theological books and commentaries before 1975, and never before the turn of the twentieth century." Kevin Giles, "The Genesis of Confusion: How 'Complementarians' Have Corrupted Communication," *Priscilla Papers* 29, no.1 (2015): 23.

8. Denny Burk, "My Take-Away's [sic] from the Trinity Debate," *Denny Burk* (blog), August 10, 2016, www.dennyburk.com/my-take-aways-from-the-trinity -debate/.

9. Piper and Grudem, *Recovering*, 40.

10. Piper and Grudem, 40–41.

11. Piper and Grudem, 41.

these definitions, affirmations, and applications, the woman's "role" boils down to puffing up the man. Following his decisions. Sitting in the passenger seat. There's nothing unique or unrepeatable about her. Ironically, she cannot freely give of her *self*, as this teaching robs her of any personhood. And that is the echo of every human heart.[12] These governing principles in much of the writing that comes from CBMW about men and women do not coincide with their other statements regarding the value of women.

And this message not only robs woman of her personhood and dignity—it robs man as well. His meaningfulness is found in his ability to exercise unilateral authority over women and in upholding cultural stereotypes of so-called masculinity. While man gets to have a more robust agency, he is one dimensional. He is defined by strength *over*, and provision and protection of the woman. This doesn't challenge him to grow through fruitful communion and reciprocity. And it gives him no telos—that ultimate hope spoken of in my introduction. This reduces manhood to dominance and calls it benevolent responsibility. One wonders, with this teaching on "masculinity," where there is room for Christ's beatitudes of the poor in spirit, the mourners, the humble, the merciful, the pure in heart, the peacemakers, and the persecuted. Man's value is in his virility. Sadly, this isn't a new teaching in the church but merely an evolved, softer version of Aristotelian metaphysics of sex polarity that has permeated the teachings of those before us. That is a bit of a mouthful. What am I speaking of here? Metaphysics speak to the reality of who we are. It is a philosophical study of the nature of reality, how things are, and how they relate. Aristotle taught that man and woman are by nature opposites and that man is superior to woman. This is a sex polarity that concludes

12. For a more detailed look at the teachings of CBMW, see Aimee Byrd, *Recovering from Biblical Manhood and Womanhood* (Grand Rapids: Zondervan, 2020).

that by nature women are inferior to men in our bodies, virtue, and wisdom.[13] Woman is opposite, other—"the female is as it were a deformed male."[14] Therefore, this is a permanent inequality in which "the male is by nature fitter for command than the female."[15]

Here is a small sampling of teachings from the church fathers, Reformers, and Puritans, which fall under the Aristotelian, sex-polarity mindset that man is superior to woman in generation. This mindset extends to the areas of intelligence and virtue; therefore, man must rule over woman:

Chrysostom: "God maintained the order of each sex by dividing the business of life into two parts, and assigned the more necessary and beneficial aspects to the man and the less important, inferior matter to the woman."[16]

Augustine: "Woman was given to man, woman who was of small intelligence and who perhaps still lives more in accordance with the promptings of the inferior flesh than by superior reason. Is this why the apostle Paul does not attribute the image of God to her?" And "I cannot think of any reason for woman being made as man's helper, if we dismiss the reason of procreation."[17]

---

13. For an excellent resource on how Aristotelian sex polarity has influenced the Western mind on the concept of woman, see Prudence Allen, *The Concept of Woman*, vol. 1, *The Aristotelian Revolution, 750 BC–AD 1250* (Grand Rapids: Eerdmans, 1985).

14. Aristotle, *Generation of Animals*, 737a, 775a, in *Woman Defamed and Woman Defended: An Anthology of Medieval Texts*, ed. Alcuin Blamires, Karen Pratt, and C. W. Marx (Oxford: Clarendon, 1992), 40.

15. Aristotle, *Politics*, 1259a37, in *Women's Life in Greece and Rome*, ed. Mary R. Lefkowitz and Maureen B. Fant, 4th ed. (London: Bloomsbury, 2016), 64.

16. Chrysostom, "The Kind of Woman Who Ought to Be Taken as Wives," Text: PG 51.230, as cited from Elizabeth A. Clark, *Women in the Early Church*, Message of the Fathers, vol. 13 (Collegeville, MN: Liturgical Press, 1983), 37.

17. *De Genesi ad literam*, Text: CSEL 28, 1, 376 and 273, as cited from Clark, *Women in the Early Church*, 40, 29.

Thomas Aquinas: "As regards the individual nature, woman is defective and misbegotten, for the active force in the male seed tends to the production of a perfect likeness in the masculine sex; while the production of woman comes from a defect in the active force or from some material indisposition, or even from some external influence."[18]

John Calvin: "On this account ['God's eternal law, which has made the female sex subject to the authority of men'], all women are born that they may acknowledge themselves as inferior in consequence to the superiority of the male sex."[19]

John Knox: "Woman in her greatest perfection was made to serve and obey man. . . . That the weak, the sick, and impotent persons shall nourish and keep the whole and strong, and finally, that the foolish, mad and frantic shall govern the discrete, and give counsel to such as be sober of mind? And such be all women, compared unto man in bearing of authority. For their sight in civil regiment, is but blindness: their strength, weakness: their counsel, foolishness: and judgement, frenzy, if it be rightly considered."[20]

William Gouge: "This metaphor shows that to his wife he is as the head of a natural body, both more eminent in place, and also more excellent in dignity: by virtue of both which, he is ruler and governor of his wife."[21]

---

18. *Summa Theologica*, I, Q. 92, Art. 1, Reply to Objection 1. See also New Advent, https://www.newadvent.org/summa/1092.htm.

19. John Calvin, *Commentary on 1 Corinthians and 2 Corinthians*, vol. 20, trans. William Pringle (Grand Rapids: Baker, 2003), 358.

20. John Knox, "The First Blast of the Trumpet against the Monstrous Regiment of Women," Project Gutenberg e-book, released October 14, 2003, https://www.gutenberg.org/files/9660/9660-h/9660-h.htm (language updated from Old English by me).

21. William Gouge, *Of Domestic Duties* (1622; Kindle ed., 2012), loc. 5879–94.

This teaching and language of male superiority and female inferiority has become offensive to our contemporary ears. Even in the ancient world, as Jacob Prahlow describes, it was more complex than these quotes about women signify, "with prescriptive and lived realities rarely standing in unison. Women in Christianity held particularly 'tense' positions, as ongoing development of church order, practice, and scriptural interpretation often stood at odds with the lived experiences and practices of Christian women."[22] As I've mentioned elsewhere, "perhaps the 'published,' proscriptive texts do not give us a real-life, on-the-ground description of women. We can observe contrast between prescribed orthodoxy of gender relations and functional orthopraxy even in our own contemporary debates about men and women."[23] These harsh teachings regarding women's nature might even be polemical measures refuting the agency that they do see some women have in society and in religion. Historians looking at evidence from everyday living, such as receipts, personal letters, invitations, legal documents, or even architectural or burial inscriptions, reveal a more complete and complex picture of women's contributions and interactions, indicating that additional factors like status, location, and needs of the community factor into a woman's opportunities for education, commerce, and religious service.[24] Although, even as we present a more nuanced and well-rounded picture, "a woman's agency was typically circumscribed by men, be it her father, husband, guardian, or tutor."[25]

---

22. Jacob J. Prahlow, "Women in the Apostolic Fathers: Context," Pursuing Veritas, April 7, 2016, https://pursuingveritas.com/2016/04/07/women-in-the-apostolic-fathers-context/.

23. Aimee Byrd, *Recovering from Biblical Manhood and Womanhood: How the Church Needs to Rediscover Her Purpose* (Grand Rapids: Zondervan, 2020), 182.

24. See Lynn H. Cohick, *Women in the World of the Earliest Christians* (Grand Rapids: Baker Academic, 2009).

25. Byrd, *Recovering*, 182–83. See also, Cohick, *Women in the World*, 322–23.

And what about now? Even as contemporary women are upgraded to being made in the image of God, the meaningfulness of our sexes—our ontology even—hasn't really been examined and reformed to the metanarrative in Scripture. Rather, the same old ontology got polished and updated with this new language of "roles." Does male and female distinction center on roles that turn out to be fixed power structures, to which "the degree that a woman's influence over a man is personal and directive it will generally offend a man's good, God-given sense of responsibility and leadership, and thus controvert God's created order"?[26] Or is there something richer and more dynamic in the meaningfulness of our sexed bodies?

We are told in Genesis that both man and woman are created in the image of God (1:27). We both hold this dignity in creation as human beings. Male and female together are icons representing the triune God. Additionally, the human body and soul exist in hylomorphic unity. This is a metaphysical understanding that has been developed throughout history that recognizes "the human being as a soul/body composite identity."[27] As Prudence Allen puts it, we understand that as the image of God there are "two distinct ways of being a human being as a male and as a female."[28] This is not something we have to force under an artificial ontological framework of authority and submission or under cultural stereotypes. Providentially, both man and woman are created for communion with the triune God. Our whole ontology, or nature, is directed toward this covenantal communion. Later we will see meaningfulness in

---

26. Piper and Grudem, *Recovering*, 51.

27. Prudence Allen, *The Concept of Woman*, vol. 3, *The Search for Communion of Persons, 1500–2015* (Grand Rapids: Eerdmans, 2016), 492. This contrasts with Plato's dualistic view of the body and soul.

28. Allen, 3:464. Allen recognizes that most of us are male or female, but because of the fall, a small percentage of people, who should receive equal dignity, suffer with intersex biology.

how our very bodies in their masculinity and femininity are typological symbols of the redemptive covenantal union in Christ that brings us to this end. But we must not conflate our typology into our ontology, or nature. Men and women do not have two different natures.

Our "sexuate installation," as Julián Marías calls it, as men and women should move us toward communion of persons as we have our eyes on Christ, where we are not actualized by what roles we play, but in fostering a mutual knowledge of one another that results in dynamic, fruitful reciprocity through the giving of ourselves through our differences.[29] But there is no room for this in CBMW's definitions of "mature" masculinity and femininity. There is no dynamism because it's all about male power, male say-so, and male agency. Complementarianism, as they name it, only boils down to who's in charge.[30]

A DIFFERENT APPROACH

Not all Christians agreed with this Danvers vision, and a year after CBMW was founded, the Council for Biblical Equality (CBE) emerged. They also composed the "Statement on Men, Women, and Biblical Equality,"[31] which argues from Scripture that "the Bible teaches the full equality of men and women in Creation and in Redemption (Gen 1:26–28, 2:23, 5:1–2; I Cor

---

29. Paul. A Zancanaro, "Julián Marías on the Empirical Structure of Human Life and Its Sexuate Condition," *International Philosophical Quarterly* 23 (December 1983): 425–40, www.pdcnet.org/ipq/content/ipq_1983_0023_0004_0425_0440?-file_type=pdf; and Julián Marías, *Metaphysical Anthropology: The Empirical Structure of Human Life* (University Park, PA: Penn State University Press, 1971).

30. Piper and Grudem, *Recovering*, 40.

31. "Statement on Men, Women, and Biblical Equality," CBE International, accessed June 10, 2021, https://www.cbeinternational.org/content/statement-men-women-and-biblical-equality.

11:11–12; Gal 3:13, 28, 5:1)."[32] This equality, they argue, is shown in full and equal partnership in mutuality in marriage, service in the church according to their gifts, and in community. CBE teaches that there is no prescribed hierarchy or ontological roles of authority between men and women. They focus on giftedness of the person, male or female, and mutuality in service. This does lend itself to a greater respect for personhood.

There is much debate in the church about women in leadership. While I do not align with the movement of complementarian teaching, I do think there is something important represented in ordination. But this book isn't really about who can enter into a calling and vocation that 98 percent of the church does not occupy, even as there are some important applications there. My focus in writing is on men and women as disciples and, in this book, how the meaningfulness of our sexes undergirds our discipleship.

Aside from the disagreement in these important areas of ordination that will continue to be debated, one critique of CBE's work is that they do not adequately address what is distinct between the sexes. But, like it or not, that isn't a part of their mission and values.[33] They were not formed so much to talk about the meaningfulness of being created male and female as they were to affirm sexual difference in equality. This is called egalitarianism. Interestingly, it was egalitarians who first spoke of complementarity between the sexes, saying that man and woman together make up the completeness of humanity. CBMW later adapted the term for their own movement, repurposing it to refer to male/female roles of headship and submission.[34] Despite the critiques of the new complemen-

32. "Statement on Men, Women, and Biblical Equality."
33. "CBE's Mission and Values," CBE International, accessed June 10, 2021, https://www.cbeinternational.org/content/cbes-mission.
34. See Giles, "Genesis of Confusion," 6–7, https://www.cbeinternational.org/sites/default/files/pp291_5tgoc_2.pdf.

tarians, egalitarians do uphold distinction between the sexes. But, again, addressing these distinctions is not a focus of their work. And when they do, it is not satisfactory to CBMW complementarians because they deny male hierarchy and female submission as an ontological role of the sexes. Even so, we are left with the question of what it means to be a man or a woman created in the image of God.

But here's the issue. Even as CBMW promotes male hierarchy and CBE promotes equality between the sexes, both organizations are speaking of what it means to be male and female in regard to what we can and cannot do. Granted, both speak of male and female being created in the image of God, but the meaningfulness of this seems to boil down to power dynamics. Power dynamics are real in every relationship and need to be addressed. I am particularly grateful for the work CBE does to expose and combat abuse. And although I am not an egalitarian, I do appreciate the work by CBE to promote the woman's voice in the church, as well as the voices of people from all ethnicities and classes. But isn't there something richer about sexual distinction than rights and equality? And even if everyone saw "biblical equality" CBE's way, wouldn't we still be asking what it means to be a man and what it means to be a woman? How is that distinction meaningful? What can we all come together and say about this? And how does that affect our discipleship?

RESPONDING TO
THE SEXUAL REVOLUTION

Men and women in the church are still confused about our sexuality. The very fact that CBMW and CBE are thriving parachurch organizations reveals this. Would Christians need to buy books, read journals, and listen to speakers talk so much about what so-called biblical manhood and womanhood is if we had a good grasp on our sexuality? And would we be arguing so much about equality and rights if we all felt like our contributions mattered in the church? Why is this?

Well, one reason is that the culture around us is confused about our sexuality and is promoting unbiblical messages about it. This is where an organization like CBMW appears to be helpful. And surely, Christians have responded to the most harmful teachings from the sexual revolution, including gender fluidity, promiscuity, homosexuality, and pornography. We know something is very wrong. But that's just it. Instead of being a model to the surrounding culture of the beauty of God's design of male and female image bearers, the church is in response mode. And in response mode, it is easy to be led by fear. The morals of our culture are dramatically shifting, and we rightfully see this as damaging to our society.

In addressing rightness and wrongness about sexuality, we can easily lose track of the meaningfulness behind it. Then a subtle shift happens. Much of our teaching on sexuality is now led by our morality rather than by the person and work of Jesus Christ. Sure, he's represented in our Christian message—but more as a fixer. We miss his very presence with his people as the resurrected Christ. Instead of seeing him going before us, still surprising us while powerfully speaking through his Word in the church, we see him as a pioneer of our ideologies as we place his words in our categories.

With the eruption of the sexual revolution in the 1960s, many in the church reacted by saying that we just needed to recapture what we had before then. The culture was stirring up a message of sexual liberation from the confines of marriage and even from the confines of our own bodies. But as Rachel Hills put it, "The 1950s weren't as buttoned up as we like to think." In an article for *TIME*, she explained how the sexual revolution associated with the 1960s and '70s "was more an incremental evolution: set in motion as much by the publication of Marie Stopes's *Married Love* in 1918, or the discovery that penicillin could be used to treat syphilis in 1943, as it was by the FDA's approval of the Pill in 1960."[35]

The sexual gender tropes of the 1950s weren't exactly biblical either. We don't see in Scripture a guide for "housewives" to put on a little makeup before their husbands come home from their day at the office, to have a delicious meal ready for them, and to stroke their egos and remove their shoes while pretending to be interested in their day. Betty Friedan was actually onto something when she addressed "the problem that has no name" in her bestselling book from the early 1960s *The Feminine Mystique*. She saw something real in challenging the 1950s ideal that "fulfillment as a woman had only one definition for American women after 1949—the housewife-mother."[36] This ideal, too, is one dimensional. She woke up America, in a sense, with the notion that women are people too, that there is much more to femininity than ironing shirts and changing the bedsheets twice a week. Sure, there is much to argue regarding some of the consequences of her work. The sexual revolution later hijacked the women's movement that she pioneered.[37] And Friedan joined it. But Christians should have a good answer to the problem that has no name, right? If more than three million copies of Friedan's book were sold in its first three years in print, maybe women were searching for the meaning behind their sex. Certainly our faith is not so fragile that it cannot rec-

35. Rachel Hills, "What Every Generation Gets Wrong about Sex," *TIME*, December 2, 2014, https://time.com/3611781/sexual-revolution-revisited/.

36. Betty Friedan, *The Feminine Mystique*, 50th anniversary ed. (London: Norton: 2013), 92.

37. To read more about this see Sue Ellen Browder, *Subverted: How I Helped the Sexual Revolution Hijack the Women's Movement* (San Francisco: Ignatius, 2015).

ognize there were some serious problems with how the culture was stereotyping men and women. And yet the church was so intertwined with the ideal image of masculinity and femininity promoted by 1950s culture that a book like Friedan's put them in response mode. Maybe the church also had some work to do while the women's movement was birthing and then being swept away by the sexual revolution.

Men and women in the church needed guidance. Marriages were affected. The family itself seemed under attack. How could men and women be fulfilled? An evangelical response came in another bestselling book by a woman: Marabel Morgan's *The Total Woman*.[38] The title sounds great, very confident. The solution to troubled marriages, Morgan taught in her book, was for the wife to be under her husband's rule. While she didn't directly address Friedan's nameless problem, Morgan had a bit of an existential crisis of her own. She said that the problem was that women need an attitude adjustment—we women become shrews.[39] We have the power to become the Total Woman by submitting to our husband's rule, puffing up his ego, keeping his home a palace that he is eager to return to after a hard day's work, and having lots of exciting sex with him so that he is comforted and never becomes bored. She has women consider our "curb appeal" to our husbands.[40] After all, he is surrounded most of the day "at the office by dazzling secretaries who emit clouds of perfume."[41] The Total Woman turns out to be June Cleaver who also transforms into a "smoldering sexpot" in surprise costumes when she meets her husband at the door.[42] "A Total Woman is not just a good housekeeper; she is a warm, loving homemaker. She is not merely a submissive sex partner;

---

38. Marabel Morgan, *The Total Woman* (Old Tappan, NJ: Revell, 1973).
39. Morgan, 21, 25.
40. Morgan, 92.
41. Morgan, 92.
42. Morgan, 95.

she is a sizzling lover. She is not just a nanny to her children; she is a woman who inspires them to reach out and up."[43]

The Total Woman was the bestselling nonfiction book in 1974. For as many who have read the book, I have yet to meet a real Total Woman as described. Apparently, Morgan is one. But notice, she is defined by her roles (and a very unrealistic fulfillment of them). This was the message to women struggling to find meaning amid a brimming sexual revolution. The problem with no name? The problem is that they weren't submissive enough, weren't sexy enough, and had not manufactured enough canned charisma for their men. I'm still trying to figure out what the kids thought when Mama met Daddy at the door in a sexed-up cowgirl outfit.

As troubling as some of this may sound, there was a shift in language. Women were no longer called the "inferior" sex, which had so long been their demarcation. And yet they were still to be ruled over. A woman's meaningfulness was in finding and keeping her man, directing his eyes to her instead of all the temptations outside the household. But don't fret; she is told that she must first be "filled" with Christ before she can be fulfilled as a woman, whatever that means. And what does this teaching tell us about men? As Kristin Kobes Du Mez put it, "*The Total Woman* offered Christians a model of femininity, but it also presented, along the way, a model of masculinity. To be a man was to have a fragile ego and a vigorous libido. Men were entitled to lead, to rule, and to have needs met—all their needs, on their terms. Morgan's version of femininity hinges on this view of masculinity."[44]

What would lead to this message selling millions of copies of *The Total Woman* and many similar books, sermons, and teachings thereafter? Fear. Evangelical women were up against

43. Morgan, 183.
44. Kristin Kobes Du Mez, *Jesus and John Wayne* (New York: Liveright, 2020), 64.

a common enemy—feminism and the sexual revolution. This was the message to help keep their families together.

And that is part of the appeal of CBMW as well. By 1977 theologian George Knight III wrote a book that helped evangelical Christians escape the language of male superiority and female inferiority and introduced this popular language of "equal but different" "roles" between the sexes that is still in use today.[45] Men and women are equal before God, yet these ontological, fixed roles distinguish men as rulers over women. CBMW later names this teaching "complementarianism." And this movement also had a common enemy, what they called "evangelical feminism." The battleground is still cracking in the church to this day to get to the meaning of being created male and female. In CBMW's groundbreaking book *Recovering Biblical Manhood and Womanhood: A Response to Evangelical Feminism*, which won *Christianity Today*'s "Book of the Year" in 1992, the case is made that their teaching on male and female roles/virtues are crucial for upholding the inerrancy of Scripture and faithfulness to the gospel.[46] That is quite a claim!

Like the secular culture, we are turning ourselves inward as we talk about sexuality. Rather than the hylomorphic unity I spoke of above, it's up to us to *put on* this so-called attribute of masculinity or femininity. While striving for a "biblical" manhood and womanhood, we've reduced our mission. We've reduced our telos, which is communion with the triune God and one another. And we've missed what Pope John Paul II called the very "glory of the human body before God" and the "glory of God in the human body, through which masculinity and femininity are manifested."[47]

---

45. George Knight III, *New Testament Teaching on the Role Relationship of Men and Women* (Grand Rapids: Baker, 1977).

46. Piper and Grudem, *Recovering*, xii.

47. See John Paul II, *Man and Woman*, TOB 57:3, 353.

WE NEED A SEXUAL REFORMATION

The sexual revolution is still going strong. And the church is still operating in reactive mode when it comes to sexuality. We still haven't really arrived at the meaningfulness of our sexed bodies. We still haven't gotten beyond power dynamics. We are still mangled up in cultural stereotypes. I have only briefly touched on the last seventy years in American history, with some recognition of what we inherited from our Christian forefathers. Our concept of man and woman has been spurious throughout world history.[48] Isn't there something more lasting and evocative to our design as men and women? Does Scripture have anything to say about this?

It most certainly does. This is why I believe we need a sexual reformation in the church. I'm not talking about a capital-R Reformation. I'm not saying that we've missed salvation itself. But the driving force of the early Reformers was a call for the church to reform according to the Scriptures. Retrieving the work of the saints before them, examining it in light of the Word of God, and applying it to the corruption of the church, they were catholic (universal) in their aim for renewal. I'm calling for a small-r reformation in the church regarding the way we understand what the Holy Spirit is saying to the churches about our sexuality.

Why should I make such a bold claim? Of course there are going to be misunderstandings in need of correction, but do we really need a reformation? When do we use that language? John Calvin noted when writing about the need for reformation in the church, "First, then, the question is not, Whether

---

48. For an excellent history on this see, Sister Prudence Allen, *The Concept of Woman*, 3 vols. (Grand Rapids: Eerdmans, 1985–2016); vol. 1, *The Aristotelian Revolution, 750 BC–AD 1250* (1985); vol. 2, *The Early Humanist Reformation, 1250–1500* (2002); vol. 3, *The Search for Communion of Persons, 1500–2015* (2016).

the Church labors under diseases both numerous and grievous (this is admitted even by all moderate judges), but whether the diseases are of a kind the cure of which admits not of longer delay, and as to which, therefore, it is neither useful nor becoming to await the result of slow remedies."[49] Here is where I stand. I stand in a culture turning further away from God. People are suffering from gender dysphoria, mutilating their bodies; women and children are objectified in pornography and film; and the horrors of sex trafficking are in the news on a regular basis. I don't merely stand in the time of the #MeToo movement, but shamefully, also the #ChurchToo movement, both revealing the depths of men abusing their power to harass and sexually assault women and children. I stand watching the church in response mode, either enacting image management or often overcorrecting with oppressive legalism, rather than showcasing the great story of Christ's love for his bride. Barry Webb offers corrective words when commenting on the degradation of women in Judges: "The church needs to be reminded of these things again and again if it is to impact the world about it in an authentically Christian way instead of capitulating to it. A church that merely plays catch up to its ambient culture will increasingly have nothing to say to that culture, and in the end, no reason to exist."[50]

Many years after the Reformation, the phrase *ecclesia reformata, semper reformanda* (the church reformed, always reforming) developed.[51] Because of our proclivity to sin and corruption, the church continuously needs to evaluate our

49. John Calvin, "The Necessity of Reforming the Church," Monergism, originally published in 1543, accessed September 16, 2020, https://www.monergism.com/thethreshold/sdg/calvin_necessityreform.html.

50. Barry G. Webb, *The Book of Judges*, NICOT (Grand Rapids: Eerdmans, 2012), 67.

51. For a history of how this developed, see R. Scott Clark, "Always Abusing Semper Reformanda," Ligonier Ministries, *Tabletalk Magazine*, November 1, 2014, https://www.ligonier.org/learn/articles/always-abusing-semper-reformanda/.

proclamations, theology, and actions according to Scripture. Because of corruption and sin, we will always be reforming, in a sense. But do we still believe this? If we do, we shouldn't be shocked to find that we have major blind spots in the church and have unintentionally adapted some of our own cultural baggage in the way we read and apply Scripture now. Often our goals in talking about sexuality in the church are way too small. And it reveals how we are letting the culture guide us, define the terms, and dictate the conversation. We have classes and curriculums about sexuality that focus on the sin of homosexuality and the distortion of transgenderism and teach "Don't have sex before marriage" and "Abortion is wrong." It is right to care about these issues, but we need to look at what is behind them. Why are they so weighty? Why are these the issues in our culture—and in our churches?

Is what it means to be a male or female image bearer of God reduced to these issues? We know this is not so. As the enemy is tirelessly working to deceive Christ's people, he aims to go after the very picture of Christ's love for his church told by the bodies of men and women. The church needs to wake up and see that we need a sexual reformation, one that isn't teaching from the other side of the same cultural coin that reduces our sexuality and robs us of our personhood. We need to direct our eyes to Christ and his exclusive love for his bride. We need to give the church Christ, and all these things will fall into place. It's time for a sexual reformation in the church.

We need to begin with Christ's spousal love for his bride. When we get that, when we know that, then we see our masculinity and femininity expressing this order of love and beckoning the beloved to Mount Zion. And there is a book right in Scripture that puts this whole story together for us. Let's look together at God's living Word to his people, particularly the Song he gives us to sing.

QUESTIONS FOR DISCUSSION

1. Why did you pick up this book to read? What are you hoping to get out of it?
2. What messages have you received from the church regarding the meaningfulness of your sex as a man or woman and your contribution to the body of Christ?
3. How do you think having an eschatological focus and imagination affects the way you view the church and live your everyday life in the midst of its cultural challenges?

Chapter Two

WE ARE SINGING THE WRONG SONG

What is the impetus behind our cultural sexual *revolution*? What drives it forward? Could it concern the same questions of meaning and value that we are asking in the church? We see men and women looking for identity in sexual pleasure, sexual expression, and even in what we can and cannot do in the church. Flowing out of this, more questions emerge about how we view our own bodies, our personhood, our neighbor, desire, and desire's ultimate satisfaction. As opposed to a revolution, a sexual *reformation* looks to God's Word as it has been read, interpreted, and confessed by his church.

The church is singing a song of worn-out lines that denies men and women the richness of their sexuality. While the church addresses sexual sin with her teaching on ontological roles, singing about so-called biblical manhood and womanhood, or even conversely promoting equality and rights, she is missing the big picture. And this picture is something that really makes us want to sing. Scripture gives us the Song of all songs. Right smack in the middle of our Bibles, we have an erotic song, the Song of Songs, which sets us in motion. Few preachers preach on it, and many who do preach on it miss the mark. What do we do with the Song of Songs? I propose that the Song of Songs is a sexual reformation call for the church, analogically enfleshing and revealing the whole metanarrative of Scripture. It reveals our deepest longing for communion with God and one another and why we even sing at all. It's an evangelical song. In it we learn about the meaningfulness of our sexuality. Our sexuality itself is a powerful analogy teaching us about the spousal love of God for his people. In addition, we can go to the Song even in our pain and suffering and experience the presence of Christ with his people. What is the Holy Spirit saying to the churches today with the Song of Songs? He is revealing much through the bride in this Song that we still have to learn.

When going through a personal crisis, we often and rightfully turn to the Scriptures for comfort and guidance. I found myself in this position when my reputation was being publicly slandered. In this trial, I felt a deep pain of betrayal, as well as a longing to be truly known. It brought me to God's Word. But when I shared with friends about the section of Scripture in which I found solace, I got some blank stares. *How in the world is Aimee finding comfort in the Song of Songs?* Talking to fellow Christians about the Song provoked some of the same reactions one might get opening up a Bible at the workplace— awkwardness. Spiritual awkwardness. *You're not going to get all weird on me, are you?* awkwardness. *How could a line like "Your eyes are doves" [Song 1:15] comfort someone in a real-life way? What does that even mean?*

Recently the Song was even made a satire piece that was shared during Valentine's Day. Imagine if your heart candies said, "Ur tower nose is hawt."[1] Okay, that's kind of funny. Is that supposed to be romantic? Some of the poetry in this song may not get the same effect as it did in its ancient Near Eastern days.

---

1. Staff, "Song of Solomon Sweetheart Candies Now Available," The Babylon Bee, February 13, 2020, https://babylonbee.com/news/song-of-solomon-sweetheart-candies-now-available.

It is meant to be provocative. And that's just the thing—the thing that kept the awkwardness in the room without moving to real conversation about it—what is this book of the Bible really about? It's a book of Scripture full of highly erotic language. *Aimee must be into some weird stuff to find comfort there.*

As I began quoting from the Song, as I will continue to refer to it, accompanied with an explanation of its meaning to offer comfort to others going through their own trials, they responded with a sense of wonder. But my friends also responded with suspicion: *In a way this sounds too good to be true. Is that really what the Song is saying?* In my own pain, I found myself escaping *in* the Song. I emphasize "in" because I really did escape there; I was in the song. *Maybe Aimee really is weird,* you're likely thinking. Perhaps a C. S. Lewis quote will help me out: "We do not want merely to see beauty, though, God knows, even that is bounty enough. We want something else which can hardly be put into words—to be united with the beauty we see, to pass into it, to receive it into ourselves, to bathe in it, to become part of it."[2] To sing the Song is to have a taste of heaven, to be *in* the beauty, to experience intimate presence with Christ. But I don't want to give all that away too early.

Jewish rabbis traditionally interpreted the Song as an allegory of God's love for Israel. While the Song is placed right smack in the middle of our Bibles, in the Hebrew Bible it had a significant placement as the first of the five scrolls, or the five *megillot*. These "writings" were read at the major festivals, the Song being read at Passover. Until the nineteenth century, the Song was interpreted by Christians as an allegory of the love of Christ for his collective bride, the church, and also for the love of Christ for the soul of the individual believer. Modern scholars and pastors began critiquing this reading, saying that

---

2. C. S. Lewis, "The Weight of Glory," in *The Weight of Glory and Other Addresses* (1949; repr., New York: HarperOne, 1980), 42.

the early interpreters were avoiding the obviously sensual and erotic language of the Song, allegorizing it to deter from what the Song plainly teaches about virginity, sex, and marriage.

I remember that early in my marriage our small group did a Song of Songs study in which we listened to sermons on cassette tapes[3] from Pastor Tommy Nelson all about the art of attraction, dating, intimacy, and conflict. The promises for the perfect marriage and sex life are all right there, we were told. Well, sign me up for the how-to on love and mind-blowing married sex! But as we listened to the tapes and had our discussions, something fell flat for me. Sure, there was plain sense application there, and I wanted to follow that, but it seemed like we were missing something even bigger. Is the main teaching for singles to remain virgins until married? Is that all there is to that? What do singles have that is valuable for contribution and communion as unmarried, whole people? It is somewhat understandable to look to the Song for teaching on love and sex, as the eroticism of the Song is undeniable. And there is certainly application there for us. But the Song is not an epistle, narrative, or how-to manual. In all this, we are forgetting that this is a song, and songs are meant to be sung. Songs have their own artfulness. Good songs have layers of meaning to them, which is why many types of people can sing along. They aren't flattened to a mere *Idiot's Guide to Marriage and Sex*.

THE SUPERLATIVE SONG

And yet the Song of Songs isn't merely a song; it is a song that is a whole book in the canon of Scripture. And it isn't just a song

---

3. Yes, I'm dating myself here!

that made it into the canon of God's inspired Word; it is the Song of all songs. Yes, even in the title, given to us in the first line, we see that this is the superlative Song, better than any other song ever sung! If we keep to just the songs of the Old Testament, then it is better than the song Moses and Miriam sang after crossing the Red Sea (Ex. 15:1–21), better than the royal wedding song in Psalm 45, better than the song of the vineyard in Isaiah 5, better than the song of Deborah and Barak (Judg. 5)—I could go on, but I've made my point.[4] Why is the Song superlative to all these? As pastor Liam Goligher answers, "Because it brings us into the holy of holies, into the presence of the One who is called the King of Kings and Lord of Lords."[5] The Song takes us—sings us—to our eschatological hope. If you want meaningfulness, the Song has it!

Do you think of the Song that way? If you do, then you will turn to it for comfort when having doubts, going through trials, and even more so, just to sing with the bride the best Song there is in complete joy. The Song's earliest interpreters didn't stumble over reading it like we do. Rather, they looked to the Song as a hermeneutical key to help solve other theological questions.[6] But later in church history, the Song of Songs gained competing interpretations regarding its genre, who wrote it, when it was written, how to read it, whether it is secular or sacred, how many male figures are in it, and even if it is a unified song or a collection of songs/poems put together. No wonder so few pastors preach on it today and we

---

4. Gregory of Nyssa also makes this point in *Gregory of Nyssa: Homilies on the Song of Songs*, trans. Richard A. Norris Jr., ed. Brian E. Daley and John T. Fitzgerald (Atlanta: Society of Biblical Literature, 2012), 29.

5. Liam Goligher, "Song of Solomon 1:1–4," The Song of Songs of the King of Kings sermon series, Tenth Presbyterian Church, January 21, 2018, https://www.tenth.org/resource-library/sermons/song-of-songs.

6. Karl Shuve, "The Song of Songs and the Fashioning of Identity in Early Latin Christianity," Academia, 2016, 2, https://www.academia.edu/14070850/The_Song_of_Songs_and_the_Fashioning_of_Identity_in_Early_Latin_Christianity.

now see much less written about it on a popular level for us to grow spiritually.

But there it is right in the middle of our Bibles. What is the Holy Spirit saying to our churches in this Song? I propose that he uses the bride to teach us why we sing at all. In it we learn all about what it really is to be loved, all about desire, all about beauty, the meaningfulness of our sexuality, and our own identity as the bride of Christ. Within this Song about Christ the Bridegroom's love for his people, the lyrics reveal a typology[7] in God's design of man and woman, one that unfolds throughout the canon of Scripture. This is the Song we want to hit repeat on. We find ourselves in it. We participate in it. We escape in it. We persevere by it. It changes us. This song is eschatological, enfleshing the metanarrative of Scripture. And as it plays in our minds, hearts, and souls, it is meant to be sung in our exhortations, prayers, and encouragement to one another.

This book invites the reader to embrace the intimate presence of Christ with his people. It is the Song he gives us in the night (Job 35:10) when we don't think he is there. It's a song of longing and a song of praise. It is why we even like music at all. We find fulfillment in it, and it transforms us. As a result, we find ourselves in the chorus, singing the Song to one another in the communion of the saints. With all the tribalism and division in the church today, we would benefit from studying the Song of Songs. And for a church in need of a sexual reformation, it makes a lot of sense to turn to what this impactful book in the canon of God's Word is teaching about our dignity and personhood before our Bridegroom.

---

7. Mitchell Chase defines a type as "a person, event, or institution that prefigures an antitype (the person or thing foreshadowed in the type)" in Mitchell L. Chase, *40 Questions about Typology and Allegory* (Grand Rapids: Kregel Academic, 2020), 36.

THE HOLY OF HOLIES

Have I hyped it up well enough? I assure you that I am not exaggerating here. Rabbi Akiva, a leading sage and tanna (teacher) in the latter first and early second centuries, passionately responded to challenges over the Song's canonicity, declaring, "'Heaven forbid! No one in Israel ever suggested that Song of Songs was not canonical. For the entire world is not as precious as the day upon which the Song of Songs was given to Israel, for all of the writings are holy and Song of Songs is the Holy of Holies! If there was a controversy, it was only concerning Ecclesiastes.'"[8] This was the classical view of the Song as well, with both Origen and Gregory of Nyssa referring to the Song as the holy of holies. In his first homily on the Song, Gregory of Nyssa invited, "Let us then come within the holy of holies, that is, the Song of Songs. For we are taught by this superlative form of expression that there is a superabundant concentration of holiness within the holy of holies, and in the same way the exalted Word promises to teach us mysteries of mysteries by the agency of the Song of Songs."[9] The Song brings us into the most intimate communion with Christ. Right away, in the fourth verse of the Song, the woman asserts, "Take me with you—let's hurry. Oh, that the king would bring me to his chambers." And just like the boy in the novel and movie *The Neverending Story*, we readers find ourselves incorporated into the Song as we are taken behind the veil to the inner chamber, where we long to "get in."

Even though there is a lot we do not know about the Song, it gives us eyes to see God's love for his people by evoking all our other senses as well. And as we see ourselves as the bride:

---

8. T. Yadayim 2:14, quoted in Reuven Hammer, "Akiva and the Song of Songs," in *Akiva: Life, Legend, Legacy* (Lincoln: University of Nebraska Press, 2015), 96, www.jstor.org/stable/j.ctt1d98bb4.12.

9. Gregory of Nyssa, *Gregory of Nyssa*, 29.

"We are beholders of the Beholder's beholding of us."[10] Like Adam and Eve before the fall, we are naked and unashamed before the Lord. But this is even more glorious than creation, because unlike Adam, our Groom is the very one who took our shame and gave us himself and all his blessings. The Song, then, doesn't merely take us back to creation. It enfleshes the meta-narrative of the whole canon of Scripture, which is still moving us to our telos. And it gives us a peek behind the veil, where we experience the intimate presence of Christ and join our voices with the bride, singing, "Maranatha!" (1 Cor. 16:22; Rev. 22:17, 20).[11] In the Song, we get a taste of what we all long for and for which our bodies, created as man and woman, speak. It reveals what Pope John Paul II called the "dignity of the human body, which is organically connected with the freedom of the gift of person in the integral authenticity of its personal subjectivity, male or female."[12] I know this is a mouthful. But the content of what he is saying will unfold in the following chapters. The takeaway for now is that our bodies hold a grandeur of worth before God and to one another. This is the meaning we are searching for. You see, I'm not exaggerating here—this is the good stuff! We will expand on this in the next chapter.

READING THE SONG CHRISTIANLY

So how are we to read this Song? We are to read it as a part of the canon of Scripture. And we read Scripture differently

---

10. Amy Brown Hughes, "Beholding the Beholder," in *Trinity without Hierarchy: Reclaiming Nicene Orthodoxy in Evangelical Theology*, ed. Michael Bird and Scott Harrower (Grand Rapids: Kregel, 2019), 131.

11. See Christopher Mitchell, *The Song of Songs*, Concordia Commentary (St. Louis, MO: Concordia, 2003), 258.

12. John Paul II, *Man and Woman He Created Them: A Theology of the Body*, trans. Michael Waldstein (Boston: Pauline Books & Media, 1986, 2006), TOB 58:6, 359.

than other books. Sure, like other books, we read each book of the Bible according to the genre in which it is written. And here we have song and poetry. But unlike regular books, we aren't the ones "standing over" the text, rationally engaging with it, per se. We are "sitting under," reading the living Word of God to his people. As Scott Swain explains, "We are instead rational subjects addressed by the divine Subject and called to loving attention and fellowship."[13] We read Scripture as God's people—Christians. We are receiving his Word, which authorizes us to listen and obey. As God's *people*, we aren't isolated readers but are part of a historical interpretive community of people. This helps us in interpretation as we have the parameters of our creeds and confessions of faith to serve as guardrails for us. As responsible readers, we also look to how the church has read the Song throughout history.

We can look at the canon of Scripture as a covenant treaty initiating a covenant community. Our transcendent creator God communicates with us through covenant. His Word is promise. How amazing it is to consider that the triune God wants to communicate and commune with us! Revealing himself in his living Word, our mighty King not only sets forth the terms of his covenantal relationship with his people but also fulfills those terms on our behalf, delivering us from the curse of sin. Swain highlights the importance of the trinitarian and covenantal context in understanding and interpreting Scripture. He says, "The Bible is one of the preeminent means whereby the triune God communicates himself to us and holds communion with us. And biblical interpretation is one of the preeminent means whereby we draw upon the riches that God has covenanted to us in Christ and whereby we hold communion with him."[14]

---

13. Scott Swain, *Trinity, Revelation, and Reading* (New York: T&T Clark, 2011), 7.
14. Swain, 7.

What does all this mean when reading the Song? Well, the superlative Song of all of Scripture must have something to do with this covenantal communion. It can't be "flatfooted,"[15] as Paul Griffiths calls it, into merely talking about horizontal relationships, even one as meaningful as the covenantal marriage between husband and wife. We cannot begin to know the richest way to love our spouse if we do not have our desires properly oriented to our Great Lover, Jesus Christ. Is this not imperative for both singles and marrieds? "Human loves and desires, most intensely the sexual ones, figure and participate in our desire for the Lord and his for us."[16] The Song does not teach us how to perfect our marriages or single life. It teaches us how to perfect our love for Christ in a knowledge of his love for us and all that he has promised to those of us who love him.[17] I will get into this in more detail in the next chapter, but marriage enfleshes our hope, and therefore the Song enfleshes our hope with the analogical expressions of the bodies of Jesus Christ and his bride. Our bodies are "meant to sing the greatest of all songs—the Song of Songs."[18] Christopher West explains, "The Song of Songs takes us to the very heart of Christian faith. And that heart is this: we can enter into nuptial union with God, our deepest aspiration. The erotic love poetry of the Song of Songs gives us entrance to the wedding feast that never ends. It transports heaven's love song into an earthly key, enabling us to hit the notes, so to speak."[19]

Isn't this the very reason why the disciples on the road to Emmaus said that their hearts burned within them when Jesus

---

15. Paul J. Griffiths, *Song of Songs* (Grand Rapids: Brazos, 2011), 5.

16. Griffiths, 56.

17. Thank you to Anna Anderson for filling this out for me more in a personal communication.

18. Christopher West, *Our Bodies Tell God's Story: Discovering the Divine Plan for Love, Sex, and Gender* (Grand Rapids: Brazos, 2020), 119.

19. West, 122.

explained the Scriptures to them (Luke 24:32)? Just after the news of hearing that the tomb was empty and that Jesus was alive, these disciples were fretting about it all as they walked together. Jesus approached them, and preventing them from recognizing him, he asked what they were disputing about. After they explained, he rebuked them for their unbelief in all the prophets had spoken: "Then beginning with Moses and all the Prophets, he interpreted for them the things concerning himself in all the Scriptures" (Luke 24:27). It wasn't until Christ blessed and broke bread with them—and we see that language of the sacrament of the Lord's Supper: took the bread, blessed it, and broke it (Luke 22:19)—that their eyes were opened to recognize the Lord. Previously they couldn't see him in the Scriptures; now they could, and their hearts burned within them. Imagine the part on that walk when Jesus got to the Song of Songs! It concerns himself as the Bridegroom. He is the lover! An almighty flame (Song 8:6)! They, and we, are the beloved!

As Richard Hays puts it, Jesus reads backward so that the first event/meaning in an Old Testament text isn't replaced, but rather, later intertextual interpretation enlightens the reader to a retrospective recognition: "Because the two poles of a figure are events within 'the flowing stream' of time, the correspondence can be discerned only after the second event has occurred and imparted a new pattern of significance to the first. But once the pattern of correspondence has been grasped, the semantic force of the figure flows both ways, as the second event receives deeper significance from the first."[20] For example, when Paul wrote in Galatians that Sarah and Hagar were prophetic figures allegorically representing two covenants, he activated the Genesis text in a whole new way, enlightening our

---

20. Richard B. Hays, *Reading Backwards: Figural Christology and the Fourfold Gospel Witness* (Waco, TX: Baylor University Press, 2014), 3.

understanding to a much bigger picture than the plain-sense reading of the narrative first revealed (4:21–31). Prophetic, allegorical, and typological reading do not replace the first, plain-sense, reading. They give it even more significance. Craig Carter says it this way: "The human authorial intent should be understood to be the literal sense of the text, and the divine authorial intent that goes beyond conscious human intent should be understood as the extended literal sense of the text. The two are often identical, but sometimes divine authorial intent—as in messianic typology, for example—goes beyond what the human author consciously understood himself to be doing. This is the crucial difference between inspired writing and noninspired writing."[21]

Human authors and readers are in time. The divine author is not. So we should be encouraged to read Scripture theologically, looking for what the Holy Spirit is saying to the churches today in his revelatory Word.

What can we know about these people in the Song? Whether the man and the woman of the Song were real people or representative characters in the human author's intention of writing, they also prefigured the unified story that all of the canon is telling of Jesus Christ, the Bridegroom, and his bride, the collective church. Now that we have the whole canon, it's all so clear. The Bible begins and ends with a wedding. In the creation account, we read of the man bonding with his wife, becoming one flesh (Gen. 2:24). And at the end of Revelation, we are given a vision of the bride of Christ, the new Jerusalem (Rev. 21). Isaiah, Hosea, Ezekiel, and Jeremiah all spoke of marriage between God and his people.[22] The first miracle Jesus performed was at a wedding (John 2:1–11). John the Baptist called himself the best man

---

21. Craig Carter, *Contemplating God* (Grand Rapids: Baker Academic, 2021), 116.
22. I.e., Isa. 50:1; 54:5–8; 62:4–5; Jer. 2:2, 32; 3:6–24; 31:31–33; Ezek. 16; Hos. 1:2; 2:2, 14–16; 3:1–3; 9:1.

to the Bridegroom, Jesus (John 3:29–30). And Paul wrote of Christ's love for his bride, the church, saying that it is the great mystery to which our own marriages point (Eph. 5:32). It's all there! The question of human authorial intent is not given to us. It's a Song—not a narrative or an epistle. So why would we spend our energies probing into that when the typo-symbolic reading *is* the plainer reading? The Holy Spirit is speaking to us through song. And God's Word has eschatological intent to be fulfilled beyond even what the original writers of it could know due to divine authorship and the progressive nature of revelation. We *are* the bride, longing for that day of consummation and everlasting feasting. And so we are in the Song as well.

With the Song's canonical and covenantal context in mind, along with the progressive nature of revelation, we can understand that there is a story being sung in this Song. This story is God's story, and we recognize him as the interpreter of his own Word. Jesus did this for us on the road to Emmaus, teaching the disciples and us about the Word's christological focus, revealing an eschatological intent that often goes beyond the human author's immediate understanding.[23] It's all coming together. We can see an even fuller, more glorious meaning of the Song fulfilled in Christ and his love for the church. Matthew Barrett highlights how reading backward—looking for the divine authorial intent and therefore seeing the rich typology in the Bible, where the pervasive initial types in Scripture point to fulfillment and reality in their antitype—is how we can read Scripture as a unified canon.[24] He emphasizes the need to approach the text as *Christian* Scripture when we read it, meaning we will read it as gospel literature spoken by the triune God who is bringing to

---

23. Although it blows my mind how the human author wove together so much Old Testament imagery in theological perfection.

24. Matthew Barrett, *Canon, Covenant, and Christology: Rethinking Jesus and the Scriptures of Israel* (Downers Grove, IL: IVP Academic, 2020), 24–31.

fruition the very message of redemption he is communicating.[25] "Though always preserving the integrity of the many human authors, privileging the trinity of the divine author is essential because apart from such a privilege the canon's unity is driven by *pragmatics*. Instead, it should stem from a unity of *substance*."[26] Whether single, married, or divorced, struggling with pornography, promiscuity, same-sex attraction, or gender dysmorphia, we will find that meaningfulness we are looking for in that substance. Much contemporary teaching on the Song seems driven by pragmatics and misses the rich, divine melody of the Song.

Much of our contemporary commentary on the Song has failed in this way. One commentator on the Song states, "The primary target audience is the unmarried, specifically single young women.... This is a book about peer pressure at its Biblical best!"[27] This author continues that Proverbs is a book for boys, telling them to take a cold shower, and the Song is a book for girls, telling them the same. It also is advice from the bride for married women to take a warm shower.[28] Another writes, "Song of Songs is artistically and thematically lovely but not particularly theologically enriching."[29] Another says, "The Song is one of the most profane texts included in the Hebrew canon. In addition to its erotic language and themes, the name of God is nowhere mentioned or alluded to. The Song neither possesses a notion of salvation history or divine law nor offers explicit moral guidelines."[30] Let that sink in. Calling the Song a profane

---

25. Barrett, 24.

26. Barrett, 24–25, emphasis original.

27. Douglas Sean O'Donnell, *The Song of Solomon: An Invitation to Intimacy* (Wheaton, IL: Crossway, 2012), 23–24.

28. O'Donnell, 24.

29. Paul R. House, *Old Testament Theology* (Downers Grove, IL: IVP Academic, 2012), 469.

30. R. Beaton, "Song of Songs 3: History of Interpretation," in *Dictionary of the Old Testament, Wisdom, Poetry and Writings*, ed. Tremper Longman III and Peter Enns (Downers Grove, IL: InterVarsity Press, 2008), e-book, loc. 1674.

text is the same as saying there is an unsacred book in the Bible. To say it has no salvation history is the same as saying it has nothing to do with the unfolding of redemption. To say it offers no moral guidelines is to say that it has nothing to offer for our lives today.[31] To say that the Song is not theologically enriching is to say that it tells us nothing about the divine Author.

I could not disagree more. The Song of Songs is a theological song; it helps us, both men and women, single or married, to know God better. It is saturated with Old Testament imagery, echoes, and allusions. The writer of the Song didn't just know these texts but understood them and wove together all the Old Testament imagery and typology in poetic fashion. As the book of Hebrews teaches us how Jesus is the ultimate Priest, the ultimate Prophet, and the ultimate King, the Song teaches us how Jesus is the ultimate Lover. And the Song is profoundly Deuteronomic. It is the enactment of the greatest command, given in Deuteronomy 6:5, "Love the LORD your God with all your heart, with all your soul, and with all your strength."

Like the church fathers and most interpreters before the nineteenth century, I read the Song as an allegory of Christ's love for the church, as well as for the individual body and soul of the believer. This is in line with reading how Jesus taught us to read the Old Testament. But in affirming that, I do believe the church fathers sometimes veered off course a bit, falling into allegorism, trying to crack some allegorical code under every word. Rather than making leaps that the woman's breasts in the Song "point to the two sons of Aaron,"[32] we should let the text reveal its own richness in meaning through its interaction with other canonical texts through its usage of imagery,

---

31. Thanks to my friend Anna Anderson for bringing this to my attention.
32. Apponius, *The Song of Songs: Interpreted by Early Christian and Medieval Commentators*, trans. and ed. Richard A. Norris Jr., The Church's Bible, paperback ed. (Grand Rapids: Eerdmans, 2019), 165.

allusion, and typology. And modern interpreters have a point that we should not avoid the erotic language of the Song as it applies to married, sexual love between man and wife. More than one meaning lies within these magnificent lyrics. We need to avoid both allegorism and flat-footed interpretations. As Pope John Paul II said, "The content of the Song of Songs is at the same time sexual and sacred. When one prescinds from the second characteristic, one ends up treating the canticle as a purely secular, erotic composition; and when one ignores the first, one falls into allegorism. It is only by putting these two aspects together that one can read the book in the right way."[33]

Another important guideline for reading the Song is to the keep the proper distinction that the participation of the bride with the divine Bridegroom is analogical. We are not on the same plane—God is wholly other than humans. He is the Creator; we are the creatures. God does not need our love; he is not dependent on it. He is not changed by it. We are dependent on the love of the transcendent, unique, and amazingly personal triune God. It changes us. And it should draw us in complete wonder that he covenantally calls and brings his people into union with Christ through his Spirit, by grace through faith. We do not become divine; and we need that distinction ever before us. Christ's bride is in a covenantal union with him. And he is washing us clean, transforming us into his very likeness.

I cannot grasp all of this with my finite mind, but we are so loved by God that we are betrothed to the Son, being made ready for that great day when he comes to consummate this union, giving us new, glorified bodies made to worship and commune with him and one another perfectly in the new heavens and the new earth. As Sandra McCracken's song promises,

33. John Paul II, *Man and Woman*, TOB 108n97, 551.

"We will feast in the house of Zion."[34] We always have to speak analogically when we speak of God. But he reveals himself to us through his Spirit by his Word so that although we cannot know him exhaustively, we can know him truly. And to salvifically know him is to participate in the great and wonderous mystery that is Christ's love for his bride.

Of course, there is another question that lurks in the mind when wanting to read rightly. As we consider the genre and a Christian way to read it, that is, reading the Song as Scripture, we also naturally ask who the human author is.

WHO IS THE SONGWRITER?

Well, the quick answer to the question of who wrote the Song of Songs is that we will not know until that day of our glorification when we can ask the Lord ourselves. As with all of Scripture, we need to keep in mind both the divine and human authors of the text. We can be sure of one thing: it's the inspired Word of God to his church.

As for the human author the Holy Spirit worked through, the first line of the Song says, "The Song of Songs, which is Solomon's." Many have attributed authorship of the Song, along with the other wisdom books of Proverbs and Ecclesiastes, to Solomon. He is mentioned in the Song three additional times. But the title in the first verse doesn't necessarily mean that Solomon wrote the Song. As Robert Jenson notes, other possible translations could be that it is "'dedicated to Solomon' or 'about Solomon' or 'in Solomon's style,' or perhaps in yet other ways."[35] Solomon could function more as a persona.

---

34. Sandra McCracken, "We Will Feast in the House of Zion," *Psalms*, Towhee Records, 2015.

35. Robert W. Jenson, *Song of Songs* (Louisville: Westminster John Knox, 2005), 2.

His wisdom, notoriety, and kingship all come to mind when the man in the Song is associated with Solomon. Not only that, Solomon was the son of David, and his name means "peace." Perhaps even more significantly, as I just noted, the Song is the holy of holies of Scripture, and Solomon was the one qualified to build the temple. Even so, Solomon also functions as a foil in parts of the Song: the wisest man sought love in the wrong places, the one qualified to build the temple did not grasp the typology of woman as Zion,[36] the richest king did not know the "unique value of 'the one.'"[37] Some suggest that Solomon wrote this later in his life, critiquing himself. And yet literary evidence points to the Song being written centuries after Solomon's time.[38] Additionally, the Song is so steeped in Old Testament imagery, it must have been written at a time when there was a "formal or informal library anticipating a canon."[39]

But if not Solomon, who wrote the Song? I can't wait to find out in glory. Although we cannot say for sure with the evidence the church has at this point, I did want to share an interesting observation. In 1957 Israeli scholar S. D. Goitein wrote a fascinating article titled "Women as Creators of Biblical Genres," particularly focusing on women's poetry as distinct from Hebrew men's poetry. He contended that Hebrew women were very active in creating the oral literature preserved in the biblical canon, by its, as he described it, being "poured from one vessel to another."[40] Women were tradents, orally passing down the faith from one person to the next. Goitein turned to Scripture, comparing and contrasting his own observation of

---

36. See chapter 3.
37. Ellen F. Davis, *Proverbs, Ecclesiastes, and the Song of Songs* (Louisville: Westminster John Knox, 2000), 301.
38. See Davis, 239.
39. Jenson, *Song of Songs*, 4.
40. S. D. Goitein and Michael Carasik, "Women as Creators of Biblical Genres," *Prooftexts* 8, no. 1 (1988): 5, www.jstor.org/stable/20689197.

women during the first years of Israeli statehood, to show how Hebrew women participated in public life, contributing songs of lament and songs and dances of victory (often peppered with mockery). They contributed as wise women, mothers in Israel, rebukers, and prophetesses, and with love poems and wedding songs. Goitein proposed that the author of Song of Songs made use of the genre of wedding songs, giving us "one of the most beautiful creations of biblical literature."[41]

Athalya Brenner concurred with Goitein regarding female authorship of the Song, adding,

> The patriarchal bias characteristic of biblical literature in general is absent from the SoS. The female figures in it are, to a large degree, autonomous: they are linked to mothers (3:4; 6:9; 8:1–2) and "mother's sons" = "brothers" (1:6; 8:1, 8–9), but not to a "father" and his authority. . . . Female co-operation in the quest for the male lover is indicated by the appeals to and responses of the Daughters of Jerusalem chorus (2:7; 3:5; 5:8–9; 6:1, 9; 8:4). The freedom to love and express love is exploited more by the females than the males.[42]

Robert Jenson also suggests that the poet of the Song is a woman, given the point of view in which the Song is cast.[43] The woman's is the dominant voice in the Song, both opening and closing it. The dialogue between the woman and the man high-lights the mutuality of the lovers and is in parts even playful. Mark McGinnis studies the use of the first person in the Song, highlighting the dominance of the woman's usage of first-person language, over the man's, with the exception of the center

---

41. Goitein and Carasik, "Women as Creators," 19.
42. Athalya Brenner, *Sheffield Old Testament Guides: The Song of Songs* (Sheffield: Sheffield Academic, 1989), 90.
43. Jenson, *Song of Songs*, 3.

portion and climax of the Song. But "even though the woman isn't speaking," he says, "the reader feels she is present through his vivid description of her (4:1–5), his passionate desire for her (4:7–15), and his complete enrapture with her love (5:1)."[44]

Perhaps a woman is the human author of this Song. There may be some profitable implications to this worth exploring, but alas, we do not know the answer definitively. We don't need to dwell on that question. We do, however, need to heed the voice of the bride in this Song. Gregory of Nyssa refers to the bride in the Song as "the teacher."[45] If we read the Song as Scripture, and it is, then we see that the bride is indeed teaching us. And through the use of the first person perspective, the reader feels drawn into the story, sensing what she feels, as she articulates and draws out what we have always been longing for.[46] As Paul Griffiths notes, "You, whether you are male or female, are, then, identifying with the Song's beloved when you resonate with the Song's first person voice."[47]

SING WITH ME: BECOMING A STUDENT OF THE SONG

How do we learn from a Song? Like many songs, this one is not a linear narrative. It reads a lot like the book of Revelation in the sense that we are getting snapshots of scenes from different camera angles. Also like Revelation, there's an eschatological focus throughout, which helps as an interpretive key. Much of

44. Mark McGinniss, *Contributions of Selected Rhetorical Devices to a Biblical Theology of the Song of Songs* (Eugene, OR: Wipf & Stock, 2011), 33.

45. Gregory of Nyssa, *Gregory of Nyssa*, 51, and Norris's footnote, "I.e., the Bride, who in Gregory's exegesis of the Song regularly appears in the role of a mistress to her apprentices."

46. See McGinniss, *Contributions*, 18–21.

47. Griffiths, *Song of Songs*, 9.

the language is meant to evoke emotion and imagination, even as it triggers us to make connections with other uses of that language throughout Scripture. Reading it often reminds me of the way we process a dream. In fact, many commentators believe the bride is dreaming in certain parts of the Song, particularly the night scenes. And scenes in the Song often change abruptly, emphasizing themes such as absence and presence or the fecundity of garden settings versus the coldness of the city.

What is the Holy Spirit saying to churches today with the Song of Songs? We see in it that theology isn't just an intellectual pursuit of knowing the right doctrines. We experience theology in life. Both our trials and our triumphs lead us to ask, *Who is God?* And when he reveals himself to us, he is more than we could imagine. The knowledge is deeply intimate, the very flame of Yahweh (Song 8:6)! It isn't merely something to know outside of ourselves; it's how we are even *to* know ourselves. It gets into our very bones. And then we do become *united with the beauty we see. We pass into it, bathe in it, become part of it.*

To know God is to sing. I propose that the Holy Spirit is revealing much through the bride in this Song that we still have to learn. And this is very exciting! My contribution with this book merely scratches the surface of the depths of what I still have to learn. I continue to find treasures in the Song as I return to it. Many commentaries have been written on the Song throughout history. My approach is not a line-by-line commentary, but a theological look at what the bride is teaching men and women in her Song. She teaches us about our lover and about being the beloved. This is where we find our meaning and value. She teaches us about desire, reciprocal giving, radiance, peace, and perseverance. She enfleshes the metanarrative of Scripture and brings us to its consummation. She wants us to sing with her. And that is what I hope this book will lead you to do. The sexual reformation is a Song. How wonderful is that?

QUESTIONS FOR DISCUSSION

1. What has been your own personal history of how you were introduced to and taught how to read the Song of Songs? Or have you just avoided it?

2. How do you think a typological and allegorical reading of the Song informs our views about God?

3. How do you think the Song will inform our understanding of the meaningfulness of our sexes as man and woman?

Chapter Three

OUR BODIES SPEAK

If you open your Bible right in the middle, you find the Song of Songs. It's fitting to have it in the center, as the Song's melody is played out in the whole canon of Scripture. I already mentioned that the Bible opens with a wedding, the first miracle Jesus performed was at a wedding, Paul told us in Ephesians 5 about the great mystery of marriage being a typology of Christ and the church, and the Bible ends with *the* wedding. The Song is eschatological in this sense: all of us in union with Christ are awaiting that day. And in the middle of our Bibles, we have the Song of that blessed communion that awaits us, of which we may taste now. As we sing the Song, we experience together our longing, seeking, finding, and clinging to what is to come. The wedding is there! The feasting is there! And the bride is teaching us about the melody in God's whole Word and in his creation.

One pastor asked me if I am making too much out of this whole typology of the woman as the collective church/Zion. I paused for a second to consider whether I was overreacting or if he was underreacting. I concluded the latter. Matthew Barrett says, "Typology is one of the central ways—some say it is the central way—Jesus and the New Testament authors see the Old Testament fulfilled in the New Testament (e.g., 1 Cor. 10:6, 11; Rom. 5:14; 1 Peter 3:21; Heb. 8:5; 9:24)."[1] So if Paul

---

1. Matthew Barrett, *Canon, Covenant, and Christology: Rethinking Jesus and the Scriptures of Israel* (Downers Grove, IL: IVP Academic, 2020), 31.

said that a man being "joined to his wife, and the two shall become one flesh" is a profound mystery of which he is "talking about Christ and the church" (Eph. 5:31–32), he is teaching us both allegory and typology. We have this extended metaphor of Christ's love for the church pictured in human marriage, as well as man and woman as types pointing to fulfillment and reality in their antitype, Christ and his bride, the collective church. Was Paul making too much out of this typology? Was he not using the very language of the Song when he said that Christ will "present the church to himself in splendor, without spot or wrinkle or anything like that, but holy and blameless" (Eph. 5:27)? Is this not the very thing we see in Song of Songs 4:1–7, where the Groom calls attention to the bride on the day of their betrothal, proclaiming, "You are all fair, my love, And there is no spot in you" (4:7 NKJV)?

And with this bigger picture, we learn more about the creation account. Adam, as the first man made of the soil of the earth, was not good alone (Gen. 2:18). Instead of creating man and woman at the same time, God created woman from man, not from the soil of the earth, and he created her second. What is significant about this? She was the crown of creation. She was not from the soil of the earth but was an eschatological marker. When Adam saw the woman, he saw his telos, what he was to become—part of the collective bride of Christ in union with her Groom. We see in woman a typology of the church, flowing from Christ's side. And in the Song, we experience an explosion of this typology with the woman celebrating in it, teaching both women and men what it is like to be the bride of Christ. It is fitting for a woman to teach us this. As my friend Anna Anderson says, "It is our longing to love and be loved that is so much a part of who we are as the eschatological creature. It occurs to me that this Song, perhaps written by a woman, breathes the metanarrative, lives the metanarrative, enfleshes the metanarrative, gives it sounds, shapes, textures, feels, and smells like no other book of the Bible."[2] Our bodies speak! After spending significant time in the Song, I now see it all over the rest of Scripture. The intertextual references and imagery that take me back to the Song are astounding. I will get more into distinguishing the different types of literary references in chapter 6, but intertextuality in Scripture occurs when a text is referencing another section of the canon, causing a relationship between the two texts and enhancing the meaning of both. Since the sixty-six books of the Bible are part of one, unified canon with a divine author, we should even expect this.

In this chapter, I share a small sample of places I've seen the melody of the Song, along with its typology of the bride and groom. I focus more heavily on the typology of the woman/bride because I believe we've neglected this as a church. Even so, she is teaching us about our Bridegroom, and we will get to this typology of the man/groom as well. Let's begin with one of my favorites, Jesus talking with the Samaritan woman at the well in John 4:1–42. But first we need to understand the scriptural background to see how the account draws from the Song.

WOMEN, WELLS, AND WEDDINGS[3]

Where does one go today to look for a wife? There are various options—the internet, the university, the church, the local well (maybe not that last one so much). But in ancient Near Eastern society, the well is where all the good women could be found for

---

2. Anna Anderson, personal email.

3. This section originally appeared as an article for *The Mod* and is used with permission: Aimee Byrd, "Women, Wells, and Weddings," Modern Reformation, October 7, 2019, https://www.whitehorseinn.org/2019/10/the-mod-women-wells-and-weddings/.

marriage. Rebekah, Rachel, Zipporah—all well women. When a well pops up in the biblical narrative, the reader should be picking up what the Holy Spirit has been laying down: someone is about to get hitched. Common literary patterns can be seen in each well betrothal. Robert Alter connects the dots for us:

> What I would suggest is that when a biblical narrator came to the moment of his hero's betrothal, both he and his audience were aware that the scene had to unfold in particular circumstances, according to a fixed order. If some of those circumstances were altered or suppressed, or if the scene were actually omitted, that communicated something to the audience as clearly as the withered arm of our twelfth sheriff would say something to a film audience. The betrothal type-scene, then, must take place with the future bridegroom, or his surrogate, having journeyed to a foreign land. There he encounters a girl—the term *"na'arah"* invariably occurs unless the maiden is identified as so-and-so's daughter—or girls at a well. Someone, either the man or the girl, then draws water from the well; afterward, the girl or girls rush to bring home the news of the stranger's arrival (the verbs "hurry" and "run" are given recurrent emphasis at this junction of the type-scene); finally, a betrothal is concluded between the stranger and the girl, and in the majority of instances, only after he has been invited to a meal.[4]

Alter also notes how wells symbolize a woman's fertility, or female sexuality in general, referencing Proverbs 5:15–18.[5] Let's go there for a minute.

Richard Whitekettle has worked to develop this womb/

---

4. Robert Alter, *The Art of Biblical Narrative* (New York: Basic Books, 2011), 51–52.

5. Alter, 62.

wellspring homology, showing that a woman's body, in its structure and function, corresponds to the order of Levitical sacred space.[6] This is why we see all those weird purity laws associated with a woman's menstruation and postpartum discharge in Leviticus (12; 15:19–33)—her womb represents fullness of life, the inner sanctum of the divine realm. When it overflows as unbounded water, it is uninhabitable for life and a threat to sanctum, rendering her ceremonially impure for the set times (yet another pattern of familiar numbers) of seven or forty days.

In this homology, we see another literary pattern from Scripture of "creation–uncreation–re-creation" where unbounded water is confined, both with creation in Genesis 1 and the flood account in the second half of Genesis 7 and beginning of Genesis 8.[7] Literary patterns are everywhere, it seems, as we learn about the concept of woman. In the story of creation, we see an eschatological sequence where the second fills out and fructifies the first:[8]

Day and night are filled with the sun and moon for
    illumination.
The sky and sea are separated and then filled with sea
    creatures and flying creatures.
The land is separated from the sea and filled with
    vegetation, animals, and man.

6. See Richard Whitekettle, "Levitical Thought and the Feminine Reproductive Cycle: Wombs, Wellsprings, and the Primeval World," *VT* 46 (1996): 376–91. He defines homology as "an acknowledged resemblance between two objects based on perceived similarities in structure and function."

7. Whitekettle, 389. Quoting from D. J. A. Clines, "Theme in Genesis 1–11," *CBQ* 38 (1976): 499–502.

8. See Mark A. Garcia, Lecture 3.1, "Glory and the Second Human," video lecture from Theological Anthropology course, Greystone Theological Institute, accessed June 10, 2019. Themes of woman as eschatological marker, liturgical responder, and dynamic fecundity in this article are built upon in the whole of Garcia's theological anthropology course. See https://www.greystoneconnect.org/library/theological-anthropology/about/.

This pattern sets us up for the creation of the second human—woman. The original Levitical audience, knowing well the cultic necessities of sacrifice and cleansing to approach God, saw in creation of woman fullness of life. She was a liturgical partner with Adam, fructifying his word. She was an eschatological marker, as Mark Garcia describes, the crown of creation week, in which Adam saw his telos (his aim and all of ours) as joining the collective bride of Christ. She was the glory of man, picturing what we are all called to be—a "habitation of liveliness."[9] In all these ways, woman tells the story behind creation.[10] And we see what the groom sacrifices for his bride. As we are told in Genesis 2:24, man is to leave mother and father to cling to his wife. Adam, who was given the priestly vocation of guarding and keeping the garden temple, sacrificed his own body for creation of his bride. Our true Bridegroom, Jesus Christ, left fellowship with the Father in the heavenly realm to come for his bride, the church. The keeper of our souls (Ps. 121) sacrificed his own body for his bride. Fullness of life for God's image bearers is to be united to Christ as his bride. The story is all taking shape.

This is also why we see such protective laws regarding women, and even how defilement of her is associated with violating the land or the tabernacle (i.e., Deut. 24:4). Right away Adam failed as a covenant head and priest in the holy garden temple. He failed to drive out the unclean thing from the temple and passively stood by as the serpent conversed with the very embodiment of sacred space—his wife.[11] Again, the original audience would be in suspense as this was read to them. The woman had already filled out the story, adding "nor touch" to

9. Garcia, "Glory and the Second Human."

10. See Richard Bauckham, *Gospel Women: Studies of the Named Women in the Gospel* (Grand Rapids: Eerdmans, 2002), for teaching on women functioning as gynocentric interruptions to androcentric biblical texts, revealing the story behind the story.

11. See Garcia, Lecture 2.3, "The Levitical Woman," video lecture from Theological Anthropology course, Greystone Theological Institute, accessed June 10, 2019.

the command not to eat of the tree (which is parallel to the language in Lev. 11:8).[12] Uncleanliness and death abounded when she was deceived and both touched and ate. What would the high priest do now? The original audience knew there needed to be a sacrifice for sin. Would it be Adam? Would he offer himself in place of his bride?[13] There would be no offer of sacrifice from this high priest and husband. We know how this story ended.

All this built up to another well scene, this time in the New Testament. In John 4, we have one of the longest dialogues in all four gospels. Most of the elements are there, and the ones that are altered are telling us something. Jesus traveled from/to a foreign land: from Judea to Samaria of all places. He sat at a well (Jacob's well!), and there encountered his *na'arah*. Readers should already be picking up on this well betrothal narrative. But this isn't the *na'arah* they would be expecting. We learn first that she is a despised Samaritan. Later we learn about her sexual history. Jesus popped the question, only it isn't phrased like a question: "Give me a drink" (John 4:7). Instead of the woman drawing water, a theological conversation ensued. Jesus answered the woman's sarcasm about their identities by telling her about living water—the very thing her embodiment as a woman pictures. She said he didn't even have a bucket, but he knew "counsel in a person's heart is deep water; but a person of understanding draws it out" (Prov. 20:5). That's when he asked her to get her husband so she could learn that although she was like that woman passed from husband to husband in Deuteronomy 24:1–4, such that her own body, which was to represent sacred space, had been defiled and she had no real

---

12. See P. Wayne Townsend, "Eve's Answer to the Serpent: An Alternative Paradigm for Sin and Some Implications in Theology," *CTJ* 33 (1998): 399–420, https://faculty.gordon.edu/hu/bi/ted_hildebrandt/otesources/01-genesis/text/articles-books/townsend_evesanswer_ctj.pdf.

13. See L. Michael Morales, *Who Shall Ascend the Mountain of the Lord? A Biblical Theology of the Book of Leviticus*, NSBT (Downers Grove, IL: IVP, 2015), 181–84.

husband now, Jesus was the faithful Husband/High Priest. Unlike Adam, Jesus is the perfect sacrifice and would lay down his life for his bride and lead her to the heart of the divine realm—the holy of holies. He is the Bridegroom who says, "Come away, my beautiful one. For now the winter is past; the rain has ended and gone away" (Song 2:10–11).

All these cultic/priestly connotations in the well conversation (and oh how I wish I had the space to get to the picture of the mirrors and the laver in Exodus 38:8[14]) of course led the woman to ask about true worship. This defiled woman was learning that she was to be "a garden spring, a well of flowing water" (Song 4:15). The reader goes from John the Baptist talking about Jesus and saying, "He who has the bride is the groom" (John 3:29), to this betrothal scene in John 4. Jesus revealed to the woman, "I, the one speaking to you, am he" (4:26). Do we not pause from our reading and look up in awe? The disciples entered the scene dumbfounded. And what did this woman do? She made haste, leaving her water jar behind, to bring home the news of the Husband's arrival. Like the bride in Revelation, she added her voice to the Spirit's voice, saying, "Come!" (John 4:29; Rev. 22:17). And people did come. The living water was flowing. The well indeed depicted fecundity and life—even for the Samaritans. "Now many Samaritans from that town believed in him because of what the woman said" (John 4:39). And they invited him to stay. I'm sure they fed him, but we do not get the details of any feasting. Maybe this is so we can add our voices to the Spirit's and the bride's, in anticipation of the great feast that is to come.

"'Come!' Let anyone who hears, say, 'Come!' Let the one who is thirsty come. Let the one who desires take the water of life freely" (Rev. 22:17).

---

14. See Aimee Byrd, "Dignifying the Women at the Entrance," Aimee Byrd, April 23, 2021, https://aimeebyrd.com/2021/04/23/dignifying-the-women-at-the -entrance/.

PSALM 46 AND THE SONG

This imagery of the life-giving water, woman, and union of Christ and his church shows up in the Psalms as well. Maybe you would expect me to have a section on Psalm 45 and the Song. After all, that is the royal wedding song. We read the introduction to it in our Bibles, which says that it is a love song, "For the choir director: according to 'The Lilies.'" Oh my, oh my, the lilies themselves are the telltale Song of Songs sign if not the fact that it's a love song! We will get into the lilies later, but they immediately remind us of God's people, the church. And they are all over the Song. We see allusions to Psalm 45 in the Song. But that's too easy! Oh yes, "grace flows from your lips," Lord, and your Song shows us how it flows all throughout your Word to us (Ps. 45:2).

But Psalm 46 caught me by surprise. There I was, assembled with my family in front of our smart TV, ready to watch the livestream of our church's worship service during the COVID-19 lockdown in our state. The text of the sermon was Psalm 46. And as my pastor began to preach, I was astounded by how much of this psalm's language is picked up in the Song. My mind was going crazy. I began talking about it out loud to my family, to which my teens responded, "Mom, we are trying to pay attention to the sermon here." I had to hold in my thoughts until the livestream was over. That benediction through the screen sent me off in a frenzy to piece my mental notes together.

The Bride as Fortress

You will find it beneficial to stop here and read Psalm 46. My pastor started with the first verse, "God is our refuge and strength, a helper who is always found in times of trouble" (v. 1). He told us to "imagine the fortress of the thick wall and towers on the corners."[15] That's when I sat straight up with interest. At the end of the Song, the woman boldly pronounced, "I am a wall and my breasts like towers. So in his eyes I have become like one who finds peace" (Song 8:10). There's no way that's a coincidence![16] Because God is our refuge and strength, the psalm tells us, "we will not be afraid" no matter what happens on the earth, "though its water roars and foams and the mountains quake with its turmoil" (Ps. 46:2, 3). Again, I'm brought to the end of the Song! "A huge torrent cannot extinguish love; rivers cannot sweep it away" (Song 8:7). This is fascinating, as the woman is so united to Christ that his protection, life, and peace are hers.

The Flowing Streams Delighting the Bride/City of God

But I can barely gasp for thinking air as the psalm continues: "There is a river—its streams delight the city of God, the holy dwelling place of the Most High. God is within her; she will not be toppled. God will help her when the morning dawns" (Ps. 46:4–5). I can hardly believe it's all there! In the Song, both the fortress and flowing springs are typologically connected with the bride. She claims she is a wall and her breasts are towers (Song 8:10), and the Groom calls her a "garden spring, a well of flowing water streaming from Lebanon" (4:15).

This is the verse we just saw practically coming out of Jesus's mouth in conversation with the woman at the well: "Whoever drinks from the water that I give him will never get

---

15. Francis VanDelden, "Take Refuge in God," sermon, New Hope Orthodox Presbyterian Church, Frederick, MD, preached March 29, 2020, https://www.youtube.com/watch?v=QLbrK7cI6V4&t=13s.

16. What's also interesting to note is that God also calls himself a helper—the very description he uses to tell Adam what he needs in a woman. "Then the LORD God said, 'It is not good for the man to be alone. I will make a helper corresponding to him'" (Gen. 2:18). For more on woman as *ezer* and *ezer*'s military context, see Carolyn Custis James, *Half the Church: Recapturing God's Global Vision for Women* (Grand Rapids: Zondervan, 2011), and Aimee Byrd, *No Little Women: Equipping All Women in the Household of God* (Phillipsburg, NJ: P&R, 2016).

thirsty again. In fact, the water I will give him will become a well of water springing up in him for eternal life" (John 4:14). Later in John we see Jesus elaborate again: "On the last and most important day of the festival, Jesus stood up and cried out, 'If anyone is thirsty, let him come to me and drink. The one who believes in me, as the Scripture has said, will have streams of living water flow from deep within him" (7:37–38). We learn in the following verse that "he said this about the Spirit" (v. 39). And let's take this to the end of Revelation, where Jesus says, "I will freely give to the thirsty from the spring of the water of life," and where John describes, "Then he showed me the river of the water of life, clear as crystal, flowing from the throne of God and of the Lamb down the middle of the city's main street. The tree of life was on each side of the river, bearing twelve kinds of fruit, producing its fruit every month" (Rev. 21:6; 22:1–2). In Revelation we see that the "holy city, the new Jerusalem" is "prepared like a bride adorned for her husband" (21:2). This connection of the woman and the flowing water and the garden/city/temple points to the unity of the bride and the Spirit—*God is within her* (Ps. 46:5).

The Glory of Lebanon

Now let's talk about Lebanon for a moment. As we saw in Song of Songs 4:15, the woman is called a "well of flowing water streaming from Lebanon." Lebanon is mentioned seven times in the Song, symbolizing perfection (3:9; 4:8 [x2]; 4:11, 15; 5:15; 7:4). The Groom bids the woman, "Come with me from Lebanon, my bride, come with me from Lebanon!" (4:8). Ellen Davis notes how the Israelites associated Lebanon with the temple in Jerusalem. "'Lebanon' became a code word for Jerusalem's glory as God's dwelling place."[17] *The Dictionary of*

---

17. Ellen F. Davis, *Proverbs, Ecclesiastes, and the Song of Songs* (Louisville: Westminster John Knox, 2000), 267–68.

Biblical Imagery notes, "The choice and aromatic wood of the cedar of Lebanon is so synonymous with the Solomonic temple that 'Lebanon' becomes a metaphor for the temple and its glory (Ps 92:12–13; Is 60:13; Jer 22:23; Ezek 17:3, 12; cf. Sir 50:12)."[18] Not only do we see the woman called flowing water streaming *from* Lebanon in the Song, but the Groom also tells her, "The fragrance of your garments is like the fragrance of Lebanon" (4:11). Her body is continually associated with sacred space! Again, we are reminded, he *is within her.*

The Day Breaks

At the end of Psalm 46:5, we read, "God will help her when the morning dawns." We see this theme of the morning dawning in the Song. Early on, the woman exclaims, "Until the day breaks and the shadows flee, turn around, my love, and be like a gazelle or a young stag on the divided mountains" (Song 2:17). In the climax of the Song, where we see the wedding and consummation, the Groom mirrors her words back to her: "Until the day breaks and the shadows flee, I will make my way to the mountain of myrrh and the hill of frankincense" (4:6). Davis again helps us with the cultic symbolism here.

> Myrrh was the primary ingredient in the "holy anointing oil" that was liberally applied to the Temple building, its furnishing and vessels, and the priests. Frankincense was mixed with the grain offering presented by every Israelite, so the burnt offering would raise "a pleasing odor to the LORD" (Lev. 2:2). It's clear then, that the woman's personal "scent" is in fact the perfume of the Temple. The lover hastens like an eager pilgrim to the spice mountains, an image

18. Leland Ryken, James C. Wilhoit, Tremper Longman III, eds., *Dictionary of Biblical Imagery* (Downers Grove, IL: IVP Academic, 1998), 963.

that beautifully evokes the curves of a female body and the Holy Mount in Jerusalem, where the strong odors of myrrh and frankincense call to remembrance the people of Israel's intimacy with their God.[19]

He *is within her.* She is associated with the temple mountain of Jerusalem. In this highly erotic language of their wedding night, the Groom praises seven body parts of the bride in a *wasf,*[20] pointing to completion and perfection—she is the aroma, the glory (Song 4:1–7).

The Delights of the New Eden

In his sermon, my pastor mentioned the Edenic language in Psalm 46. The river with streams that delight and God dwelling with his people do echo the language of Eden. The Song, too, is full of this imagery. Phyllis Trible says it well: "Perhaps the paradise described in Genesis 2 and destroyed in Genesis 3 has been regained, expanded, and improved upon in the Song of Songs. . . . The woman is the garden (4:10–15), and to the garden her lover comes (5:1; 6:2, 11). Together they enjoy this place of sensuous delight."[21] Yes, that word *delight* is seen recurring in the Song. But the Edenic language in both Psalm 46 and the Song points us not back, but forward eschatologically to the new city/garden/temple. We see the bride presented this way in Revelation. This language is in line with what I mentioned about how the Song functions as the holy of holies of Scripture, where Christ is intimately present with his people, taking his bride and penetrating behind the veil to the inner

---

19. Davis, *Proverbs, Ecclesiastes, and the Song of Songs,* 265.

20. In ancient Arabic love poetry, *wasfs* delightfully describe multiple body parts, often using metaphoric comparisons.

21. Phyllis Trible, "Depatriarchalizing in Biblical Interpretation," *JAAR* 41, no. 1 (1973): 42–43. www.jstor.org/stable/1461386.

chamber/sanctuary. The Bridegroom brings peace to his people and to the land. And the bride joins her voice to the Spirit's, beckoning her brothers and sisters to "come."

The Formidable Bride

And there is more! Twice in the Psalm 46 we see this refrain: "The LORD of Armies is with us; the God of Jacob is our stronghold" (vv. 7, 11). Twice in the Song we see that the woman is "awe-inspiring as an army with banners" (Song 6:4, 10). She is formidable! Is it not because the God of Jacob, the God of the covenant, is her stronghold? Are we not reminded of this in John 4, where Jesus used language from the Song while he met with the woman at Jacob's well? My pastor referenced Hebrews 6:17–19, "Because God wanted to show his unchangeable purpose even more clearly to the heirs of the promise, he guaranteed it with an oath, so that through two unchangeable things, in which it is impossible for God to lie, we who have fled for refuge might have strong encouragement to seize the hope set before us. We have this hope as an anchor for the soul, firm and secure. It enters the inner sanctuary behind the curtain." There we are again, ushered behind the curtain to the inner chamber by our Groom. He binds himself to us in his covenant. What a story our bodies tell!

JOHN'S USE OF THE SONG IN HIS RESURRECTION NARRATIVE

Just two weeks after this livestream sermon on Psalm 46, my pastor preached his first Easter sermon to a quarantining congregation. He preached on the resurrection account in John 20. Now, I wasn't expecting another experience like the other week so soon, again seeing the Song of Songs everywhere, along with Revelation connections. But it does make sense, as I am finding that John, the beloved disciple, was quite the singer of the Song. And so it happened again. My mind was reeling, so back to my computer I went after that benediction, with the allusions pouring out in a sort of stream-of-consciousness style.

The Searching Bride

It was the first Easter morning, but Christ's people didn't know it yet. All they knew was that the tomb was empty. They were still experiencing darkness, like the dreaming bride in the night scenes of the Song, searching for clues. While it was so early that it was still dark, Mary Magdalene came to the tomb and discovered that the stone was rolled away! *Where is he?* Where was the One whom her soul loved? That's what the bride in the Song asked. She sought him but did not find him (3:2). Mary Magdalene ran to the disciples, frantically reporting that she did not know where they put him (John 20:2). They all ran back and found the linen cloths lying there, along with the wrapping that once was around Jesus's head, now folded and set aside (John 20:3–10). *Where is he?* Where was the One whom her soul loved (Song 3:3)? Mary didn't know it was Easter morning, bursting with the spring of new life, for she was still experiencing darkness. She and the other women had not heard the Bridegroom sing the song in the night to his love: "Arise, my darling. Come away, my beautiful one. For now, the winter is past; the rain has ended and gone away" (Song 2:10–11). They did not have the understanding to sing out in response, "Until the day breaks and the shadows flee, turn around, my love, and be like a gazelle or a young stag on the divided mountains" (Song 2:17).

The disciples returned to where Mary found them, but Mary stayed outside the tomb, crying. This is where I want to bring up the lilies again. As Havilah Dharamraj notes, Israel self-identified "as a 'lily' and a 'dove,' both familiar images in the Song." She references 4 Ezra 5:23–26, "dated to the end of the first century CE," as the first documentation of this.[22] Much earlier we see that the bride in the Song identifies herself as "a lily of the valleys" (2:1) and the Groom mirrors her, saying, "Like a lily among thorns, so is my darling among young women" (2:2). Mary Magdalene fills out the picture of the seeking bride here (Song 3:1; 5:6). She is a picture of Christ's church. But she was not in a dark city night scene. She was in a garden at daybreak. And she was a lily to her Groom, the risen Christ. She should have known that "he feeds among the lilies" (Song 2:16). He was with her all along.

The Lord is with his people. That's where Mary would find him. Or rather, he found her. "My love has gone down to his garden, to beds of spice, to feed in the gardens and gather lilies. I am my love's and my love is mine; he feeds among the lilies" (Song 6:2–3). The Bridegroom was there. He asked her why she was crying and whom she was seeking. She mistook him for the gardener (John 20:14–15). Ah yes, the gardener—*he is the Gardener!* There was the Groom—the second Adam—standing in his garden. What a picture for us! We see hints of Eden, and proleptic, or anticipatory, notions to the true city/garden/temple, the typology of which the bride herself points (Rev. 21). It's like the future breaking into the present. And what a reminder for us now that he feeds among the lilies! Christ is with his church.

---

22. Havilah Dharamraj, *Altogether Lovely: A Thematic and Intertextual Reading of the Song of Songs* (Minneapolis: Fortress, 2018), 2–3. She footnotes 4 Ezra 5:23–26: "'My Lord, my Master,' I said, 'out of all the forests of the earth, and all their trees, you have chosen one vine; from all the lands in the whole world you have chosen one plot; and out of all the flowers in the whole world you have chosen one lily. From all the depths of the sea you have filled one stream for yourself, and of all the cities ever built you have set Zion apart as your own. From all the birds that were created you have named one dove, and from all the animals that were fashioned you have taken one sheep.'" Translated by Jeremy Knapp, https://tinyurl.com/ycs6yrfe.

The Clinging Bride

"Mary," he called her by name. Ah, recognition! *It is him!* She found the One she loved, held on to him, and would not let him go (Song 3:4). Of course she would! But it was not the right time. She could not take him to her mother's house, Zion—the chamber of the one who conceived her (Song 3:4).[23] Jesus told her, "'Don't cling to me . . . since I have not yet ascended to . . . my Father and your Father, to my God and your God" (John 20:17). That time will come for the bride, but not yet. Not yet (Rev. 12).

The Bride Who Finds Peace

We will get back to Mary, but first a quick fast-forward to after she announced the good news. Jesus sought out the other disciples. Ah, how the bride fails. We sleep. We sin. We seek but cannot find. But the Groom will come to her, to us. The disciples were gathered together with the doors locked out of fear of persecution. They did not even need to rise to open for their Love (Song 5:5). He appeared, not with condemnation, but proclaiming, "Peace be with you. . . . Peace be with you" (John 20:19, 21). Oh, how their guts must have stirred within them (Song 5:4)![24] The bride had found peace! The bride is a fortress who finds her peace in the Groom's eyes (Song 8:10). He breathed on the disciples, telling them to receive the Spirit, for he was coming. Of course! In the beginning of the Song, the Groom tells his bride that she has dove's eyes (Song 1:15). When he sees her, he sees his own Spirit, represented by the dove (John 1:32).[25] He is present with her. The dove/turtledove is mentioned seven times in the Song, describing mainly the bride but also the Groom's eyes and spring in the land.

---

23. Thanks to my friend Anna Anderson for pointing out this connection to me.
24. See Davis, *Proverbs, Ecclesiastes, and the Song of Songs*, 277, on how Song 5:4 echoes Jer. 31:20, where God is saying his guts heave and churn for Ephraim.
25. Also, it was the dove that brought the olive leaf back to Noah (Gen. 8:11).

The Lord of armies, who is our refuge (Ps. 46:1), brings peace by his Spirit. Christ is the true Solomon. The son of David. The King of Peace.

The bride/Shulammite *is* Jerusalem/*Shalem*, peace, the feminine of Solomon. But nowhere else in Scripture do we see this specific reference to a Shulammite (Song 6:13). Perhaps *Shalem* is combined here with the two Shunammite women mentioned in Scripture.[26] We have the Shunammite woman in 2 Kings 4:8–37, whom Elijah promised would embrace a son. She did give birth to a son, and later when he died, she sought out Elijah and clung to him, holding him to his promise that she would have a son, and so he brought him back to life (this possibly points to Jerusalem's children restored from living death after the exile,[27] but also points us to Rev. 12). Also, there's the Shunammite woman, Abishag, in 1 Kings 1–2, the young, beautiful caretaker of David through his dying days. In this narrative, the Shunammite seemed to be both a victim or pawn of royal power and accompaniment or accent to it, as Adonijah tried manipulating his brother Solomon for a bid to the throne by acquiring her for marriage. He convinced Solomon's mother, Bathsheba, to make a request to Solomon for Adonijah to marry her. Solomon saw through the manipulation and killed him for it. Davis, again, has great insight here on the contrast in the Song and how that may activate and critique the 1 Kings 1-2 text. Our Shulammite in the Song is not merely an accompaniment to power; she "embodies power. Ultimately, with her lover the 'king' (7:5, see also 1:4, 12), she calls into question royal pretentions to power (8:11–12). Thus she represents *the incorporation and integrity of power*—in a woman, in a united people, in a soul unified in its devotion to one 'Beloved'

---

26. Davis makes this point in *Proverbs, Ecclesiastes, and the Song of Songs*, 289–91.

27. See Davis, 291.

(vv. 10–13)."[28] In these combinations of Jerusalem/feminine of Solomon/Shunammite, we have the Shulammite, the city of peace associated with woman at peace.

She calls herself a fortress, saying, "I am a wall and my breasts like towers. So in his eyes I have become like one who finds peace" (Song 8:10).

The Commissioned Bride

It may not be time to cling to the Groom yet, but it is time to spread the good news! He tells the Shulammite, "You who dwell in the gardens, companions are listening for your voice; let me hear you!" (Song 8:13). "Mary Magdalene went and announced to the disciples, 'I have seen the Lord!' And she told them what he had said to her" (John 20:18). After appearing to the other disciples, Jesus sent them as well to spread the good news of the forgiveness of sins (John 20:21–23). The Bridegroom brings peace to his people. And the bride joins her voice to the Spirit's, beckoning her brothers and sisters to "come" (Rev. 22:17).

"He who testifies about these things says, 'Yes, I am coming soon.' Amen! Come, Lord Jesus!" (Rev. 22:20). "Run away with me, my love, and be like a gazelle or a young stag on the mountains of spices" (Song 8:14).

SING WITH ME

These are but a few examples of intertextual echoes and allusions in and to the Song. But why does all this matter? It matters because, as Christopher West puts it in the title of his book, our bodies tell God's story.[29] Too often we think of our bodies

---

28. Davis, 291, emphasis original.
29. Christopher West, *Our Bodies Tell God's Story: Discovering the Divine Plan for Love, Sex, and Gender* (Grand Rapids: Brazos, 2020).

as less than our souls, which are the truest part of us. The sexual revolution has capitalized on this mindset. Our bodies are reduced and objectified, sex becomes entertainment, and our gender becomes our choice. And yet, we are full of pain, abuse, and dysfunction. This isn't the story our bodies are supposed to tell. Many are very confused about the meaningfulness of our bodies, both as unrepeatable human beings and as distinctly male and female. We live in a time when gender dysphoria is rising, as the mindset is that our souls can have a different sex than our bodies. Children are being injected with hormones and having their bodies mutilated to try and change their sex. But it doesn't take away their pain. In her work *The Concept of Woman*, Roman Catholic philosopher Sister Prudence Allen rescues the historical, metaphysical understanding that recognizes "the human being as a soul/body composite identity."[30] Our souls and bodies belong together as one identity; that is how we are made.

Our Bodies Speak

When God made us in his image, he gave us bodies and souls—"he created them male and female" (Gen. 1:27). He is the Creator; we are the created image bearers. God is spirit and does not have a body,[31] and yet he gave us bodies to image him. Why did he do this? What do our bodies speak? In the incarnation, Jesus took on human flesh to be our mediator of the new covenant. That's how much he cares about our bodies. He was born of a woman (Gal. 4:4). Christ didn't just come to save our souls, but to be the firstfruits of the resurrection so that we, too, will be raised with new bodies upon his second coming

---

30. Prudence Allen, *The Concept of Woman*, vol. 3, *The Search for Communion of Persons, 1500–2015* (Grand Rapids: Eerdmans, 2016), 492. This contrasts with Plato's dualistic view of the body and soul.

31. See Westminster Confession of Faith 2.1.

(1 Cor. 15:20). We will be given eternal bodies. Our bodies matter to God, and they should matter to us. They speak, making visible the invisible, the marital story of Christ's spousal love for his bride and the eternal communion we will share with him on the new heavens and the new earth.[32]

And the Song enfleshes this metanarrative. In it we see the distinction between the man and the woman, as well as communion through giving of the self in and through these differences. We will get more into the gift language in chapter 5. Right now I want to get into the melody. Do you hear the melody of what we are supposed to be? It is the bride who sings it! And in the Song, the Groom bids us to look at her. In the center of the Song, when we are bidden to gaze at the King on his wedding day, the Groom immediately points us to the bride. He poetically praises her beauty in *wasf* form, praising seven parts of her body. Perfection! And yet this description leads us no closer to knowing what she actually looks like. We instead are given imagery of what her body evokes. The Groom uses temple language as he delights in her. Her hair portrays livelihood and movement streaming from Mount Gilead, a holy place for Israel's history.[33] Her lips, like a scarlet cord, remind us of holy garments.[34] Her brow is like a slice of pomegranate, which were embroidered on the priest's robes.[35] She is likened to the mountain of myrrh, the temple mount of Jerusalem,[36] and he will make his way to the mountain. She *is* the holy edifice and the bride. Why is this? Because he *is within her!* The bride is joined to the Spirit. To behold her is to behold "the holy city, the new Jerusalem, coming down out of heaven from God,

---

32. See West, *Our Bodies*, 11–16.
33. See 1 Sam. 13.
34. See Ex. 28:5, 6, 8, 33.
35. Ex. 28: 33.
36. 2 Chron. 3:1; known as the mountain of myrrh because of the incense burned at its temple services.

prepared like a bride adorned for her husband" (Rev. 21:2). Like the Proverbs 31 woman, she is the glory of her husband (v. 23). That's the thing about beauty, isn't it? It speaks. As Robert Jenson suggests, "Beauty is realized eschatology, the present glow of the sheer goodness that will be at the end."[37]

Woman's Prophetic Meaning

And this matters because what's true of the bride is true of us. She tells the story behind the story for the beloved of Christ. Clement of Rome put it this way when writing about Rahab: "Ye see, dearly beloved, not only faith, but prophecy, is found in the woman."[38] Pope John Paul II emphasized that in Paul's revealing of the mystery of marriage in Ephesians, he "enables us to think of a special kind of 'prophetism' that belongs to women in their femininity. The analogy of the Bridegroom and the Bride speaks of the love with which every human being—man and woman—is loved by God in Christ. But in the context of the biblical analogy and the text's interior logic, it is precisely the woman—the bride—who manifests this truth to everyone."[39] And so the Song is prophetic as well. It grabs the lyrics from creation and the imagery of the prophets and enfleshes them in man and woman to sing of our groaning now and the rhapsody that is to come. We see much of this story in the typology of the woman.

Woman reveals the endgame. We were created to be the covenantal bride of Christ. She is an embodiment of eschatological glory. We see woman's distinct glory from man in dynamic, synergetic, fructifying of the Word. And the typology of the

---

37. Robert W. Jenson, *Song of Songs* (Louisville: Westminster John Knox, 2005), 46.

38. 1 Clem. 12:8.

39. John Paul II, *Mulieris Dignitatem*, apostolic letter, August 15, 1988, §29, http://www.vatican.va/content/john-paul-ii/en/apost_letters/1988/documents/hf_jp-ii_apl_19880815_mulieris-dignitatem.html.

bride endgame is showcased in Revelation 21:11 and 22:17, prophetically adding her voice to the Spirit's, calling her brothers to perseverance to come to the water of life, of which her whole body is a homology. In her we see the responsibility of laymen and laywomen, as the bride of Christ, to hear and speak the testimony of Jesus, spurring one another to wakefulness and perseverance.

Male and Female Love

There are layers of meaning and application to this story that our bodies tell. We should be led to worshipful praise of our Groom as we spur on one another. Our theology isn't mere doctrine on how to get right with God but is saturated in erotic love language that brings us into delightful communion with him. As we learn about the love of God, we are in awe of him. And as we behold him, we learn about ourselves and even our sexuality. We learn about male and female love and can grow in understanding of how that should look on the ground. Again, Pope John Paul II was helpful here:

> *Christ is the Bridegroom.* This expresses the truth about the love of God who "first loved us" (cf. 1 Jn 4:19) and who, with the gift generated by this spousal love for man, has exceeded all human expectations: "He loved them to the end" (Jn 13:1). The Bridegroom—the Son consubstantial with the Father as God—became the son of Mary; he became the "son of man", true man, a male. *The symbol of the Bridegroom is masculine.* This masculine symbol represents the human aspect of the divine love which God has for Israel, for the Church, and for all people. Meditating on what the Gospels say about Christ's attitude towards women, we can conclude that *as a man,* a son of Israel, *he revealed* the dignity of the "daughters of Abraham" (cf. Lk 13:16), *the dignity belonging to women*

from the very "beginning" on an equal footing with men. At the same time Christ emphasized the originality which distinguishes women from men, all the richness lavished upon women in the mystery of creation. Christ's attitude towards women serves as a model of what the Letter to the Ephesians expresses with the concept of "bridegroom". Precisely because Christ's divine love is the love of a Bridegroom, it is the model and pattern of all human love, men's love in particular.[40]

Isn't this beautiful? Does it not make your soul sing? Pope John Paul II explained how the Bridegroom is the lover and the bride is the beloved. The very dignity of the woman is measured in this order of love.[41] It is a reciprocal love, as she wears, fructifies, and returns man's love. We see this foremost in the spousal love of Christ. And that transforms the way we see ourselves and love others. Yes, it will certainly teach us in our marriages. But since Christ is our ultimate Bridegroom, the Song is for singles, divorcees, and widows, as it is ultimately moving us closer into our vertical relationship with God. All of our bodies speak about this love. Unmarrieds tell this story with their bodies as well. Single women's bodies also point to the wellspring of life! They testify to the coming Messiah. Single men still model this order of love in a platonic fashion when they honor and dignify women. The Song is for those who suffer with gender dysphoria, those born intersexed, and those struggling with same-sex attraction. It's for those of us who are insecure with our bodies and for those suffering with body dysmorphia. Even as we suffer from the effects of the fall, our bodies still speak. Sometimes they groan and lament, asking

---

40. John Paul II, *Mulieris Dignitatem*, §25, emphasis original.
41. John Paul II, *Mulieris Dignitatem*, §29.

the Lord, "How long?" (Ps. 13:1). Even then, our bodies are loved. They are meant to glorify Christ. He gives his people dignity and fulfillment in longing. We will get more into desire and recognizing ourselves and one another as gifts in the following chapters. Even those who have been emotionally, physically, and sexually abused—the Song is for you too. All of us need to know the great Lover of our bodies and souls, Jesus Christ. He gives us our value and meaningfulness.

And Christ's bride—all the collective people who make up his bride—is a locked garden (Song 4:12). Nineteenth-century preacher Charles Spurgeon explained it this way, "But it is a garden enclosed, and so enclosed that one cannot see over its walls so shut out from the world's wilderness, that the passer -by must not enter it—so protected from all intrusion that it is a guarded Paradise—as secret as was that inner place, the holy of holies, within the tabernacle of old."[42] We are talking the holy of holies kind of love and presence here! Our love must be properly oriented, first vertically in Christ, and then in its appropriate expression as brothers and sisters or in eros and agape love in marriage between a man and a woman.

While the church rightfully upholds family values, a caution is in order for improper orientation in our teaching. If our focus is on the horizontal relationships—chastity for singles, love between a husband and wife, and biological sex and gender congruency—we fail to grasp why it matters. When we lose the story that our bodies speak, we fall into legalism. We lose love; we lose Christ. Our affections and our teaching must be first oriented vertically to our great love story. And it isn't just a story. We are seeking Christ's presence in his Word to his church. This is where we find true power to love others well,

---

42. Charles Haddon Spurgeon, "A Secret and Yet No Secret (SS 4:12 & 14)," in *Charles Spurgeon on the Song of Solomon: 64 Sermons to Ignite a Passion for Jesus!* Christian Classics Treasury (2013), Kindle ed., loc. 7990.

to recognize lust as an evil counterfeit, to mortify sin, and even to endure suffering.

There is an already-and-not-yet truth welling up inside of us. Christians are given new life in the Spirit, so we experience a taste of this communion in the holy of holies. But we await its consummation, so it is partially hidden to the world and even in our own reality now. As our bodies are temples of the living God inhabited by his Spirit, we mediate his presence to the world, his love flowing out of us. We all are feminine in the sense that we are the receivers of God's love. And now in our respective, distinct bodies, we spread its fragrance. Our bodies speak. So speak the truth. No, sing it!

QUESTIONS FOR DISCUSSION

1. How did the intertextual references and echoes I pointed out between the Song of Songs and other Scripture passages activate the text they were alluding to, enhancing the meaning of both texts?

2. How does this typology of woman as Zion/bride and the analogies of woman as fortress, water of life, and Lebanon elevate the dignity of women from the way the church has historically described them?

3. How would an understanding of the typology of man and woman as it relates to the divine order of love be applied to our relationships in the church? How does that affect the way you think about leadership and the value of laymen and laywomen as disciples and disciplers?

Chapter Four

THE WOMAN'S DESIRE AND THE DESIROUS WOMAN

We don't often use the word *desire* in everyday language. It comes off pretty strong and usually has sexual connotations. In the Old Testament, we see a rare Hebrew word, *teshuqah*, used only three times, translated as "desire." It means "stretching out after, a longing—desire."[1] It comes from the root word *shuq*, which can mean "to run after" or "overflow."[2] Actually, it isn't that simple; the word has various interpretations. *Teshuqah* is associated with woman in two out of its three occurrences. First, directly after the fall when God declared the consequences: "He said to the woman: 'I will intensify your labor pains; you will bear children with painful effort. Your *desire* will be for your husband, yet he will rule over you'" (Gen. 3:16, emphasis added). And then when the bride in the Song is speaking about her Groom: "I am my love's, and his *desire* is for me" (Song 7:10, emphasis added).

The other time we see this word is when God addressed Cain before he murdered his brother: "If you do what is right,

---

1. James Strong, *The New Strong's Exhaustive Concordance of the Bible* (Nashville: Thomas Nelson, 1990), 262, 126.
2. Strong, 114.

won't you be accepted? But if you do not do what is right, sin is crouching at the door. Its *desire* is for you, but you must rule over it" (Gen. 4:7, emphasis added). The variations of what this desire means are wide, particularly when it comes to Genesis 3:16 and the woman's desire. The ancient Greek version of the Old Testament, the Septuagint (LXX), gives the meaning a bit more nuance, translating *teshuqah* as *apostrophē*, meaning a "turning" or "returning" toward her husband. This is interesting because another Greek word, *epithumia*, would have translated more closely to the meaning of "desire." Some commentators have even suggested this was a clerical error.[3] Jerome's Vulgate, a Latin translation, is quite surprising in that the woman's desire or turning is absent—taking out her agency altogether—with Genesis 3:16c and d mirroring one another: "You will be under the power of your husband, and he will rule over you."

Later commentators have varied on whether to focus their interpretations according to the etymology of the word, the context within its particular text, or how it relates in the other two places it's used. Some use a narrow meaning, saying the woman will still sexually desire her husband even though she will suffer pain in childbirth; some say she will still long for marriage and the intimacies that go with it despite the husband's rule; some think this means that the woman will submit her "desires" to her husband; and others see it as a single-minded devotion to her husband. These were the main views out of a variety of interpretations before Susan Foh and her research while at Westminster Theological Seminary came along. She outlined three of these views in her journal article[4]

---

3. Joel N. Lohr, "Sexual Desire? Eve, Genesis 3:16, and תשוקה," *JBL* 130 (2011): 231.

4. Susan T. Foh, "What Is the Woman's Desire?," *WTJ* 37 (1974/75): 376–83, http://faculty.gordon.edu/hu/bi/ted_hildebrandt/OTeSources/01-Genesis/Text/Articles-Books/Foh-WomansDesire-WTJ.pdf.

that presents a novel interpretation of the woman's desire. It is curious that Foh's interpretation is now the consensus of many contemporary scholars. It changes the way we view woman and her relationship to man.

Foh, who was later associated with the beginning of the movement of biblical manhood and womanhood,[5] made such an impact in her innovative interpretation that it even led to new Bible translations, such as the ESV's, "To the woman he said, '. . . Your desire shall be contrary to your husband, but he shall rule over you.'"[6] Did you catch that? The woman's desire isn't *for* her husband anymore—it is sinfully *contrary to* her husband. A large consensus of modern-day, like-minded commentators now interpret Genesis 3:16cd as meaning that since the fall, women's desire is a power lust over men. Therefore, husbands need to take caution, as their wives are continuously trying to usurp their "authority." Woman wants to dominate man, and she must be stopped by his ruling over her. In comparing Genesis 4:7 with Genesis 3:16, paralleling *woman* to *sin* in the passage, Susan Foh pioneered this interpretation:[7]

The woman has the same sort of desire for her husband that sin has for Cain, a desire to possess or control him. This desire disputes the headship of the husband. As the Lord

5. Council on Biblical Manhood and Womanhood, "Our History," cbmw.org, https://cbmw.org/about/history/.

6. See also the New Living Translation: "And you will desire to control your husband, but he will rule over you," and the NET Bible, "You will want to control your husband, but he will dominate you."

7. Kendra Dahl shows evidence in her paper written for Westminster Seminary California, "The Gracious Continuity of the Woman's Desire: An Analysis of Susan's Foh's Interpretation of Genesis 3:16 and an Alternate Proposal," that one other commentator, P. Joüon, took this view in 1908. But since Joüon's article is in French and she could not locate it, she needed to rely on A. A. Macintosh, "The Meaning of Hebrew תשוקה," *JSS* 61 (Autumn 2016): 384. Dahl notes how interesting it is that Joüon did not get the support that Foh did, possibly due to the social situation of second-wave feminism in which Foh's contemporaries were responding.

tells Cain what he should do, i.e., master or rule sin, the Lord also states what the husband should do, rule over his wife. . . . The woman's desire is to control her husband, to usurp his divinely appointed headship, and he must master her, if he can. So the rule of love founded in paradise is replaced by struggle, tyranny and domination.[8]

"WHAT IS THE WOMAN'S DESIRE?"

This question is the title of Susan Foh's infamous journal article, written in the mid-1970s. This was a time when the church was responding to second-wave feminism and when the church seemed to be in battle with the woman's desire. Leading up to Foh, some other commentators of this passage also emphasized an Aristotelian view of women's baser appetites. Keil and Delitzsch, while upholding a form of Aristotelian male superiority even before the fall, claim that woman's sin led to her "enfeebling of nature," interpreting her pronounced desire as "bordering upon disease" and "a violent craving for a thing."[9]

One may think that Foh's interpretation would be right in line with what we've seen quoted by the church fathers and any commentators taking their lead, according to some of the quotes I shared earlier on their views about women and the Aristotelian sex-polarity context they operated under.[10] And yet, even as a reading of Genesis 3:16 in a manner like Foh's may have served their own philosophical leanings about women, none of them interpreted it the way that she did. As one commentator reminds us,

8. Foh, "What Is the Woman's Desire?," 381–82.

9. Carl Friedrich Keil and Franz Delitzsch, *Commentaries on the Old Testament*, vol. 1, *The Pentateuch* (Grand Rapids: Eerdmans, 1949), 103.

10. See chapter 1, pp. 4–5.

Of the twelve known ancient versions (the Greek Septuagint, the Syriac Peshitta, the Samaritan Pentateuch, the Old Latin, the Sahidic, the Bohairic, the Ethiopic, the Arabic, Aquila's Greek, Symmachus's Greek, Theodotion's Greek and the Latin Vulgate), almost every one (twenty-one out of twenty-eight times) renders these three instances of *teshuqah* as "turning," not "desire."

Likewise, the church fathers (Clement of Rome, Irenaeus, Tertullian, Origen, Epiphanius and Jerome, along with Philo, a Jew who died about A.D. 50) seem to be ignorant of any other sense for this word *teshuqah* than the translation of "turning." Furthermore, the Latin rendering was *conversio* and the Greek was *apostrophē* or *epistrophē*, words all meaning "a turning."[11]

Rather than a lust for power over the man, the church fathers who wrote on this verse, such as Origen, Chrysostom, Didymus, Ambrose, and Augustine understood the woman's desire as a positive "turning" toward him.[12] And they interpreted the husband's rule as benevolent. For example, Origen preached that the husband shall be his wife's refuge.[13] This is also in line with the Genesis account in the book of Jubilees (second century BCE), which, as Joel Lohr points out, "uses the term *megba'*," meaning "'place of refuge,' or 'place of return.' . . . In Jub. 3:24, therefore, Eve is told, 'Your place of refuge will be with your husband; he will rule over you.' The same term is used in the Ethiopic version of Genesis in both 3:16 and 4:7.26."[14]

---

11. Walter Kaiser et al., "3:16 How was the Woman Punished?," in Walter C. Kaiser Jr., Peter H. Davids, F. F. Bruce, and Manfred Brauch, *Hard Sayings of the Bible*, The Hard Sayings series (Downers Grove, IL: InterVarsity Press, 1996), 66.

12. Lohr, "Sexual Desire?," 238–40.

13. Origen, *Homilies on Genesis and Exodus*, ed. Ronald E. Heine (Baltimore: Catholic University of America Press, 2010), 122.

14. Lohr, "Sexual Desire?," 232–33, cites his dependance on James C. VanderKam, *The Book of Jubilees*, 2 vols., CSCO 510–11 (Leuven: Peeters, 1989), 1:19:

In addition to the collective interpretation and translations of ancient Jewish midrash[15] and the church fathers' referring to *teshuqah* as a positive turning and returning to its subject, Lohr examines the usage of this Hebrew word in the Qumran extrabiblical manuscripts of the Dead Sea Scrolls.[16] His findings reveal that "returning" is consistently the best interpretation of its usage. And this nuance works in all three of our Bible verses: "Despite increased pain in childbearing, Eve would actively return to the man. Cain was warned that sin (or perhaps Abel) would return to him, but he could master, or rule over, it. The woman who waited for her absent lover in Canticles was certain that her lover would return to her."[17] In this, he gives credence to the LXX's taking license by using *apostrophē* instead of *epithumia*, as he sees the nuance appropriate.

But what about the English translation "desire"? Is it wrong? Would "return" be a better translation? Lohr does concede that there may be overlapping semantic range, and as the ancients saw these words close in meaning, he speculates that *teshuqah* and *apostrophē* nuance "a strong movement toward, perhaps of an impelling nature, returning someone (or thing) to where he or she (or it) belonged, perhaps for refuge or to one's origins, or even for destruction or in the sense that the returning is final." This makes a lot of sense to me, as desire has to have an orientation. Lohr does wonder if desire worked for "older English but has since become problematic on account of its usage and connotations in a highly sexualized Western society."[18]

"For our purposes I refer only to the Ethiopic version, as the fragments from Qumran and the citations by Greek writers do not include Jub. 3:24 (the verse related to our study)."

15. Midrash is a method of Hebrew biblical interpretation and elaboration from ancient oral tradition.

16. Lohr, "Sexual Desire?," 240–46.

17. Lohr, 244.

18. Lohr, 245.

THE SPARK OF OUR DESIRE

Thus, I thought it would suit us well to look at *desire*'s modern given definition. Merriam-Webster defines desire this way:

1. conscious impulse toward something that promises enjoyment or satisfaction in its attainment
2. (a) longing, craving; (b) sexual urge or appetite
3. something longed or hoped for: something desired[19]
4. a usually formal request or petition for some action[20]

The definitions in the semantic range of the word *desire* can also work together. Certainly an "impulse toward something that promises enjoyment or satisfaction" would lead to a "longing" that would provoke something like a "request for some action." And in the different nuances of its definitional usage, we have that word "toward" that insinuates an orientation of desire, a turning. While I affirm the importance of recognizing the history of the interpretation being "turning" or "returning," I also think that "desire" adds a spark, a spark of eros even, to this turning that reveals the power of the verb—a longing in the turn, a hope for satisfaction and enjoyment, the very "stretching out after, a longing—desire" from our simple concordance definition. But as we know, this is a description after the fall, and it is anything but simple.

Phyllis Trible has an enlightening explanation of woman's desire in Genesis 3:16. She notes that this moment of the woman taking a bite of the fruit and giving it to man, who also partook, is a turning point in their one-flesh unity that was

---

19. Don't you hate it when dictionary definitions define a word using that exact word?

20. *Merriam-Webster*, s.v. "desire," accessed June 19, 2021, https://www.merriam -webster.com/dictionary/desire.

just poetically recorded in Genesis 2:24. Now they are opposed to one another. This is revealed further when Adam betrayed her when confronted by God (Gen. 3:12). Says Trible, "Yet, according to God, she still yearns for the original unity of male and female." She longs to go back to that union uninterrupted by sin. Trible adds, "The man will not reciprocate the woman's desire; instead, he will rule over her. Thus, she lives in unresolved tension. Where once there was mutuality, now there is a hierarchy of division." This division corrupts both man and woman, she says. "His supremacy is neither a divine right nor a male prerogative. Her subordination is neither a divine decree nor the female destiny. Both their positions result from shared disobedience. God describes this consequence but does not prescribe its punishment." And what a difference this is from man's first poetic, rapturous description of woman in Genesis 2:24. "Eros has disintegrated," Trible concludes.[21] This sounds similar to Lohr's returning someone (or thing) to where he or she (or it) belonged, perhaps for refuge or to one's origins.

Kendra Dahl, in concluding that Foh "reaches faulty conclusions out of a reactivity to second wave feminism," sees a "gracious continuity" that is woven through God's pronouncement of the fall. She proposes that woman's desire is "an act of God's grace and the means through which he will bring about his promised deliverer." She sees this return of desire as a restoration from what was lost from their rebellion. And yet, "this return will be marked by pain—as the woman gives birth in faith, looking to the seed to come, she also does so in pain, remembering what her sin cost." Does not the pain in childbirth point to Christ's own travail in birthing the church? It also brings pain into her marriage, marred by the consequences of sin. But as they hope for the promised seed to come, which provides for their own

---

21. Phyllis Trible, *God and Rhetoric of Sexuality*, Overtures to Biblical Theology (Philadelphia: Fortress, 1978), 128.

redemption, both the man and the woman are dependent on the grace of God, and "they can live even within their sin-stained marriage as a picture of the gospel (Eph 5:22–33)."[22]

Anna Anderson also proposes a recovery of looking at the woman's desire as good. I couldn't agree more with her assessment of the importance of how we interpret this:

> I believe that what we decide to do with the "desire" question in Genesis 3:16c has vast implications—from the rule of man in Genesis 3:16d all the way through to the wife of the lamb in Revelation 21. It will inform every appearance of the woman in the Bible. It will be the backdrop of every interaction between the husband and wife in the Bible and set the trajectory of the woman and a path to understanding her right through till the end.
>
> If Aristotle, Keil, Foh, and Wenham are right about her, the woman will be judged either as one who has overcome or as one who has succumbed to the specific diseases of her soul. If Eve has brought wasting blight upon her daughters, then all the figures of the Old Testament—the historical women of the Pentateuch, Prophets, and Writings, the woman of wisdom in Proverbs 31, the women in the gospels from Elizabeth to Mary Magdalene, and the apostolic directives in the epistles concerning women, culminating in the apocalyptic woman Jezebel and the wife of the Lamb of Revelation—all can be understood better in light of the woman plagued by desire. Her victories will be understood at least as over the woman's specific lusts, and her defeats will be in some way traceable to her distinctive desire.[23]

22. Dahl, "The Gracious Continuity of the Woman's Desire," 55, 57.
23. Anna Anderson, "Is the Woman's Desire Bad?," *Reforming Anthropology*, blog, August 17, 2020, http://reforminganthropology.com/index.php/2020/08/17/is-the-womans-desire-bad/.

Is this desire part of the curse for woman's sin, something she wears as a plague that needs to be overcome, or, as Anderson proposes, is it a marker of God's people as his bride? "In fact, the woman's desire might be something uniquely pointing not to something she needs to be redeemed *from*, but something that every one of us need to be redeemed *to* (2 Tim. 4:8). . . . Could it be that desire is something that all of us, male and female, are called to cultivate daily in our lives in light of being the eternal bride of Christ?" Anderson then moves to the Song, where we will be going soon, to make that very point. And she concludes that just as Adam's work is still good, even as the consequences of sin have corrupted the land, woman's desire is also good yet is thwarted "in a world under the reign of sin, Satan, and death." And if this is so, "then we will not see rabid lust as specifically identified and unfolded in regard to the woman, but rather thwarted and unrequited desire as a theme attached to her in the pages of Scripture. This trajectory would then consummate in a lover and his beloved who find their desires met in one another."[24]

This trajectory plunges us into the Song. And rightfully so, as the woman's desire will never ultimately be satisfied in an earthly husband. She will indeed land in despair if her turning is to him as the ultimate hope of her longings. Joy in marriage is found in a very similar way as joy in virginity. Unlike the many resources marketed to Christians today, it isn't found in so-called biblical manhood or womanhood. Unlike the many who oppose them, it isn't found in egalitarianism. Unlike what the world says, it isn't found in sexual pleasure. As Abigail Favale puts it, "The virgin represents the human being alone before God, divested of any extrinsic valuation." The virgin is "the bodily sign of the human person whose value is rooted not

---

24. Anderson, "Is the Woman's Desire Bad?"

in earthly bonds, but in Christ himself." Our sexual distinction, she says, "is not made purposeful through mandated tasks or restrictive temporal roles; the supreme meaning of our sexed natures is to be living, visible icons that gesture continually toward the world beyond the veil."[25] Joy is found in properly oriented desire. Therefore, joy in marriage will not be found in our earthly spouses or in mind-blowing monogamous sex, but in what marriage itself points to, our true Bridegroom, Jesus Christ. He is the spark of our desire. If we get that, then we have the proper gratitude and enjoyment for those gifts in singlehood and marriage, as well as the proper lamenting when rightfully oriented desires are thwarted and unrequited, and repentance when they go off course and are tainted and disoriented by our own sin and brokenness.

DESIRE FULFILLED

One reason why I think the translation "desire" is so appropriate is because of this intertextual reference in the Song. In reading Scripture, we have to ask not only "What is this text saying?" but "What is this text doing?"[26] The Word of God is living and active (Heb. 4:12), and it transforms the reader. Rosalind Clarke explains that in the Song, the reader isn't some third-party observer, but a participant who is being courted.[27] She recognizes the Song as a microcosm of the entirety of Scripture,

25. Abigail Favale, "Sex and Symbol," University of Notre Dame, Church Life Journal, June 19, 2018, https://churchlifejournal.nd.edu/articles/sex-and-symbol/?utm_content=139633573&utm_medium=social&utm_source=twitter&hss_channel=tw-938492208109555712.

26. See Rosalind S. Clarke, "Canonical Interpretations of the Song of Songs" (PhD diss., University of Aberdeen, 2013), 57, https://eu03.alma.exlibrisgroup.com/view/delivery/44ABE_INST/12152788870005941.

27. Clarke, 227.

which "begins and ends with eschatological yearning."[28] The first man and woman yearned for that eschatological blessing from God for their obedience—the union of heaven and earth and eternal communion with the triune God and one another. Scripture reveals that Jesus Christ, the second Adam, is the obedient Son who will bring us to this blessing (Rom. 5:12–21). He is the end of our desire. We see this consummated at the close of Revelation with the bride, the new Jerusalem, coming down out of heaven from God (21:2, 9–11). Reading the Song not only captures the whole story of Scripture, but it evokes that longing in us to enter into the freedom and reality of this new life in Christ. The bride opens with her desire to be kissed by the kisses of the Groom's mouth and ends the Song by calling him to the spice-laden mountains, Zion (1:2; 8:14). The Song unleashes all our senses and our imaginations to search for these gems of reality, propelling us forward to our telos. It's absolutely thrilling!

And so Clarke continues, "Desire is, above all things, the perlocutionary[29] goal of the Song, and in the context of the canon, there is nothing more to be desired than the union of the divine bridegroom with his bride."[30] Reading the Song evokes desire in us, while also giving us the proper orientation of our desire—it *turns us* to the face of Christ. In the Song, we have a glimpse of the beatific vision that is to come—desire fulfilled in beholding his transcendent glory. And on that great day, as Kyle Strobel says, we will not only see "a vision of deity, but of God as he is for me."[31] I would tweak that to, "God as he is for *me* and for *us*." Because, as we confess as a church, "I believe

---

28. Clarke, 225.

29. The effect that is enacted on the hearer by the speaking itself.

30. Clarke, "Canonical Interpretations," 235.

31. Kyle Strobel, "A Spiritual Sight of Love: Constructing a Doctrine of the Beatific Vision," Union, accessed November 10, 2020, https://www.uniontheology.org/resources/bible/biblical-theology/a-spiritual-sight-of-love-constructing-a-doctrine-of-the-beatific-vision.

in the communion of the saints."[32] Are we perhaps guilty in our theology of upholding a Savior who gave his whole life for us, but not seeing him as the Groom who absolutely desires and delights in us? In the Song, we not only see his desire, but his desire arouses our own. And we long for that day when we will consummate that desire.

The Song turns us. Yes, I already said that. But I want us to really think about this. I was speaking with my friend Anna about this concept, and she mentioned the parable of the ten virgins in Matthew 25:1–13. What's the difference between the wise virgins and the foolish ones? It's not merely being prepared with enough oil by being smart enough to consider the oil factor ahead of time. Interestingly, Rosalind Clarke gives us some insight when she talks about reading the Song in its canonical context as wisdom literature. She says that "the Song tests the wisdom of the reader."[33] Let me ask the million-dollar wisdom question: *Do we know the identity of this woman?* Her very body points us to Zion, her mother's house (Song 8:2). She is the mountains of spices to which she is calling her Groom (Song 8:14). She is the city coming down out of heaven from God, the bride of the Lamb (Rev. 21:10–11). She is the beloved of Christ! She is all of us who desire him! That is an active thing; and so, in love and wisdom, she longs for him. The absence scenes in the Song evoke that longing in all of us who identify with her. We heed, with her, the warnings to love rightly. "Do not stir up or awaken love until the appropriate time" (Song 2:7; 3:5; 8:4). And our lamps are full as we wait, because he fills them. "For the LORD gives wisdom" (Prov. 2:6). The wise virgins *longed* for the Groom. That's what they had that the foolish ones did not. They desired him.

---

32. The Apostles' Creed.
33. Clarke, "Canonical Interpretations," 237.

Why? Because, as Thomas Shepard reasons, "the Lord Jesus longs for them."[34] Look at how he prayed for us: "Father, I want those you have given me to be with me where I am, so that they will see my glory, which you have given me because you loved me before the world's foundation" (John 17:24). Shepard notes that Jesus was praying as though he were in heaven already.[35] He longed for that great day of consummation with his bride. We long for him because he first longed for us. And he is keeping us on the way (Ps. 121:4–8).

Let's play the devil's advocate like the young women in the Song for a moment: "What makes the one you love better than another, most beautiful of women? What makes him better than another, that you would give us this charge?" (Song 5:9). The wise bride answers with a *wasf* poem, praising his body from top to bottom. But when we read it, it's not exactly a description to give to the police sketch artist. Some commentators see an echo of this in John's description in the beginning of Revelation (1:12–16). Neither actually describes his looks; both use temple language in describing him.[36] Both sections describe his hair, eyes, and mouth, and use the words "white" and "gold(en)," and mention "streams" or "waters." And we read both but still have no idea what he looks like. But as Ellen Davis illuminates, the bride "uses metaphors to communicate *how she feels about him.*"[37]

---

34. Thomas Shepard, *The Parable of the Ten Virgins* (Orlando, FL: Soli Deo Gloria, 2006), 160.

35. Shepard, 160.

36. In the Song, his lips are lilies (Song 5:13, the capitals on top of the pillars were shaped like lilies [1 Kings 22]; also lilies are representative of his people); his legs are alabaster pillars (Song 5:15), possibly alluding to the pillars Boaz (meaning, "in him is strength") and Jachin (meaning, "he will establish") on the porch of Solomon's temple (1 Kings 7:15–22, 41–42; 2 Kings 25:13, 17; Jer. 52:17, 20ff.; 2 Chron. 3:15–17; 4:12–13); his presence is like Lebanon (Song 5:15). And in Revelation he is dressed in a robe, possibly that of a high priest, among the seven golden lampstands (Rev. 1:12–13). For some of these allusions, see Nick T. Batzig, "John's Use of the Song of Songs in the Book of Revelation," Feeding on Christ, July 1, 2013, https://feeding onchrist.org/johns-use-of-the-song-of-songs-in-the-book-of-revelation/.

37. Ellen F. Davis, *Proverbs, Ecclesiastes, and the Song of Songs* (Louisville:

It's not about what he looks like but who he is. She ends by saying, "He is absolutely desirable. This is my love, and this is my friend, young women of Jerusalem" (Song 5:16). What honor and value she must feel from her Groom to call him her love *and* her friend. This doesn't indicate a lustful desire to reduce her to an end to his pleasure—his relationship with her is pure and good to the core, elevating her dignity and personhood. It fructifies her. Grace flows from his lips (Ps. 45:2).

In this *wasf*, the bride says, "His lips are lilies" (Song 5:13). I love this line. We immediately remember how the lilies represent Christ's church. The Groom has already called her a "lily among thorns" (2:2). And now we are seeing a repetition of themes coming together. The bride immodestly opens the Song, longing out loud, "Oh, that he would kiss me with the kisses of his mouth!" (1:2). Now she is saying that these kissable "lips *are* lilies, dripping with flowing myrrh" (5:13, emphasis added). We've also established that myrrh is a perfume of the temple. It's as if she is saying that we, the collective church, are on his lips! This is a desire that is so intimate that it can only be expressed through such vivid and lovely poetic images. What is this text *doing* here? It is practically putting us on the lips of Christ! Does this not evoke a longing within the reader to be on those lips? To participate in this kind of beautiful intimacy? All of our senses are drawn into it: seeing the lilies, smelling them, feeling the dripping myrrh.

Let's go to that marital scene where the desire is again expressed so vividly (Song 4:1–5:1). Here the Groom praises his bride's body in *wasf* form, saying he will make his way to the mountain of myrrh (4:6), and that she has captured his heart (4:9), and she responds, "Awaken, north wind; come, south wind.

Westminster John Knox, 2000), 281, emphasis original.

Blow on my garden, and spread the fragrances of its spices. Let my love come to his garden and eat its choicest fruits" (4:16).

Wow! Can she get more sexually provocative than that? She calls the whole winds of the earth into this desire! Is she not summoning the work of the Spirit to stir the spices analogically associated with her body and set them in flight, creating the sensual feast as he did in Genesis 1 (John 3:8)?[38] Such empowerment is displayed in the woman's desire. And the Groom's response: "I have come to my garden—my sister, my bride. I gather my myrrh with my spices. I eat my honeycomb with my honey. I drink my wine with my milk" (5:1).

And in this scene of desire fulfilled, we don't see animalistic consumption of one person for the pleasure of another. We see something wonderous. This is the third time in this lovemaking scene that the Groom calls her first his sister, then his bride.[39] He honors her with dignity and value. He waits for her invitation. Pause and think about the tenderness of his desire for his bride. And his utmost respect for her. Men, please pause. Take this in. This is masculinity, as represented in Christ. We will get back to that.

Then there is this curious narrator, whom Richard Davidson recognizes as Yahweh himself,[40] pronouncing the marital blessing "as he did at the first garden wedding in Eden":[41] "Eat, friends! Drink, be intoxicated with caresses!" (5:1).

Isn't this the fulfillment in the woman/bride's "turning/

38. Observation made by Anna Anderson, personal correspondence.

39. See Song 4:9–10.

40. This is an instance of prosopological exegesis. Matthew Bates shares a basic definition, saying "prosopological exegesis—involved assigning dramatic characters to otherwise ambivalent speeches in inspired texts as an explanatory method." Matthew Bates, *The Birth of the Trinity: Jesus, God, and Spirit in New Testament and Early Christian Interpretations of the Old Testament* (Oxford: Oxford University Press, 2016), 3. What appears as an ambiguous passage is the Father's voice blessing this union.

41. Richard M. Davidson, *Flame of Yahweh: Sexuality in the Old Testament* (Grand Rapids: Baker Academic, 2007), 591.

returning"? I love how some of the church fathers connect woman's desire in Genesis 3:16 with "refuge" as we saw above. It all culminates in the Song, of course. Is there a better line in Scripture than "I am my love's, and his desire is for me" (Song 7:10)? His desire is both the means and the end of her turning. It is stronger and purer than the predatory "desire" of sin that we see directed toward man in Genesis 4:7, leading to life rather than death.[42] At the end of the Song, the bride claims that he is her refuge: "I am a wall and my breasts like towers. So in his eyes I have become like one who finds peace" (8:10). I discussed this in the last chapter. She is a fortress.

Notice the pneumatological element there in the Song. She has "dove's eyes" (1:15), and she mirrors that language back to him in the *wasf* (5:12) and then finds peace in his eyes (Song 8:10). The dove is clearly a symbol of the Spirit. As Gregory of Nyssa said, "Hence the most perfect praise of eyes is that the form of their life is shaped in conformity with the grace of the Holy Spirit, for the Holy Spirit is a dove."[43] The Spirit turns the lights on for us, gives us eyes to see, and gives us life in union with Christ. Strobel speaks of the ultimate fulfillment of this, when we reach that beatific vision in glory: "Anthropologically, the human person is fully alive in the sight of God, knowing and being known in love, and is therefore able to rest in the fullness of God's life such that he or she is able to embrace life itself."[44] In this, we see that we are known in trinitarian love, beholding the love of Father and Son by the Spirit, from which all love overflows. All love begins within the perichoretic[45] love

---

42. See Davis, *Proverbs, Ecclesiastes, and the Song of Songs*, 295.

43. Gregory of Nyssa, *Gregory of Nyssa: Homilies on the Song of Songs*, trans. Richard A. Norris Jr., ed. Brian E. Daley and John T. Fitzgerald (Atlanta: Society of Biblical Literature, 2012), 231.

44. Strobel, "A Spiritual Sight of Love."

45. Perichoresis describes the eternal, mutual indwelling union between the triune persons of the Father, Son, and Holy Spirit.

of the Trinity, the indwelling of the three eternal persons who dwell in unity, "naked and unashamed."[46]

Now, doesn't this make any other desire pale in comparison? Or as Shepard put it, "If this love be not worth longing for, truly it is worth nothing."[47] Why is this? Because we long to be truly known and delighted in. And that's what this text does. It directs our true longing. It undresses us in the context of the exclusive, covenantal love of Christ. It lifts the veil and takes us into the holy of holies. And we get to enter into his tender love, making us naked and unashamed.

THE RADIANT, DESIROUS WOMAN

The lights come on in the Song of Songs just as they do at the end of the whole story in Revelation. In both we are given a resplendent picture of the bride of Christ, radiant with his glory. The beholding of Christ's bride does something to us—it illuminates what God has in store for us and leaves us in awe of his splendor. But the text in the Song doesn't didactically teach us about the bride's identity. Its imagery and poetry provoke us to ask, *Who is this woman?* Wondrously, as she begins her bridal procession, someone—we can't be sure who—blurts out the rhetorical question we are all asking: *"Who is this coming up from the wilderness like columns of smoke, scented with myrrh and frankincense from every fragrant powder of the merchant?"* (Song 3:6).

The question itself offers some interesting clues to who she is. First of all, why is she coming out of the wilderness? This language should remind us of Israel's story of forty years in the

---

46. Thanks to Anna Anderson for making that connection back to Genesis in personal correspondence.
47. Shepard, *Parable of the Ten Virgins*, 161.

wilderness and entering the promised land.[48] We read about this connection of Israel's history with her identity as bride in Jeremiah: "Go and announce directly to Jerusalem that this is what the LORD says: I remember the loyalty of your youth, your love as a bride—how you followed me in the wilderness, in a land not sown" (Jer. 2:2, see also Hos. 2:14–15).

Something else is curious about this bride. While myrrh was a common bridal fragrance of the time (Esth. 2:12), frankincense was not. So here is something used for sacred space, added to the sacrificial offering as a "pleasing aroma to the LORD" (Lev. 6:15). And we see more tabernacle language in her "coming up" like pilgrims at the end of their journey to worship at the sanctuary (Jer. 31:6; Ps. 122:4). Thus, this is the beautiful bride of the LORD, coming up to the house of God as both the one offering the sacrifice and the sacrifice itself. How magnificent, indeed!

Revelation fills this out more for us: "Come, I will show you the bride, the wife of the Lamb" (21:9). Immediately after the angel said this, John was carried away in the Spirit "to a great, high mountain" where he saw "the holy city, Jerusalem, coming down out of heaven from God, arrayed with God's glory. Her radiance was like a precious jewel, like a jasper stone, clear as crystal" (21:10–11). What does this passage *do*? Does it not leave you in awe? It activates our text from the Song, enriching its meaning. *Who is this woman?* She is the new Jerusalem, coming down out of heaven from God, the bride of the Lamb. She is the woman, coming up from the wilderness, where the royal mother-bride (as we see in Ps. 45) has been nourished until this time (Rev. 12:6, 14).

So many metaphors are ascribed to the bride, showing her exuberance and liveliness. She is pointing us to something and

---

48. Much of my discussion on this passage comes from Davis, *Proverbs, Ecclesiastes, and the Song of Songs*, 260–61.

evoking a desire in us to go there too. This meaningfulness is showcased in the name given to the first woman. Even after the fall, by God's grace she was given the prophetic name Eve—as wife and mother of all the living. The bride in the Song alludes to this as she keeps longing to bring her Groom where they can consummate their love in the mother's house (3:4; 8:2). Also in the Song, the tower, wall, and gate imagery attributed to her body is connected to that city imagery in Revelation. Not only that, but she is "a locked garden and a sealed spring" (4:12). As Jill Munro puts it, "All the splendour and beauty of the natural world is for a moment concentrated on her."[49] Do you see it? Who she is? It all points to one typology, Zion, as both body and edifice—person and place.[50]

And she is radiant (Rev. 21:11). That word should stand out to us. She is radiant like her Groom. He is described that way in Hebrews: "The Son is the radiance of God's glory" (1:3). The bride's radiance comes from him. "Those who look to him are radiant with joy; their faces will never be ashamed" (Ps. 34:5). The Groom affirms this in the Song, calling out that same question as before, "Who is this who shines like the dawn, as beautiful as the moon, bright as the sun, awe-inspiriting as an army with banners?" (6:10). He knows who it is. He wants us to know! We are reminded again of the woman in Revelation 12, who is "clothed with the sun, with the moon under her feet and a crown of twelve stars on her head" (v. 1), and of the description of Jesus Christ in the beginning of Revelation, "He had seven stars in his right hand; a sharp, double-edged sword came from his mouth, and his face was shining like the sun at

---

49. Jill Munro, *Spikenard and Saffron: A Study in the Poetic Language of the Song of Songs* (Sheffield: Sheffield Academic Press, 1995), 51.

50. Much attribution and gratitude go to Anna Anderson for personal and email conversations in which she enlightened me on the mother language. The typology is also apparent in Isaiah 44–66.

full strength" (1:16). We can't look away! We desire to see this, to see him. *Those who look to him are radiant with joy!* That's what the beatific vision does.

It transforms us. Munro notes how strikingly different the language the Groom uses to describe his bride is from how the woman describes herself in the beginning of the Song (1:6). "There, she pleads with the daughters of Jerusalem not to look at her on account of the swarthiness of her skin which the sun has caused, literally by 'looking' at her. Now, in 6.10, the woman is identified with the clarity and strength of the sun so as to draw their gaze. She who was once despised and outcast, has become their queen."[51] She notes the preceding verse: "Women see her and declare her fortunate; queens and concubines also, and they sing her praises" (6:9).

Jesus Christ holistically transforms the bride in her whole typico-symbolic representation—person and place. This is what we hope for. In the description of the new Jerusalem, we read that "the city does not need the sun or moon to shine on it, because the glory of God illuminates it, and its lamp is the Lamb" (Rev. 21:23). His radiance turns on the lights. We see because of him.

> The sun will be no longer be your light by day,
> and the brightness of the moon will not shine on you.
> The LORD will be your everlasting light,
> and your God will be your splendor.
> Your sun will no longer set,
> and your moon will not fade;
> for the LORD will be your everlasting light,
> and the days of your sorrow will be over.
> (Isa. 60:19–20)

---

51. Munro, *Spikenard and Saffron*, 39.

> I will not keep silent because of Zion,
> and I will not keep still because of Jerusalem,
> until her righteousness shines like a bright light
> and her salvation, like a flaming torch. (Isa. 62:1)

This longing desire lights a spark that doesn't fade! But oh, others have tried. We need to sing with the bride, "Love's flames are fiery flames—an almighty flame!" (Song 8:6). You don't get any more radiant than that! Davidson notes how fire is associated with God's presence in Scripture,[52] and the Song teaches us that "coming into love is like coming into God's presence."[53] This is our desire, the fulfillment we long for. Our desire will always grow—how exciting that is to affirm—but in him we have the consummate satisfaction of an almighty flame.

THE SPOUSAL LOVE OF GOD

Earlier I said that our goals in talking about sexuality in the church are way too small, and how that reveals that we are letting the culture guide us, define the terms, and dictate the conversation. Yes, we care very much about the issues of our day, such as promiscuity, pornography, abortion, same-sex attraction, and gender dysphoria. As weighty as these issues are, we are addressing symptoms without getting to the root: what our longings are created for, where our desires should be oriented, what the meaningfulness of our sex is, and what we are living for.

We need to direct our eyes to Christ and his exclusive love

---

52. Davidson, *Flame of Yahweh*, 628. E.g., Gen. 3:24; 15:17; Ex. 3:2; 13:21; 40:38; Num. 9:15.

53. Davidson, 628, quoting from George M. Schwab, *The Song of Songs' Cautionary Message concerning Human Love* (New York: Peter Lang, 2002), 63.

for his bride. We need to give the church Christ, and all these things will fall into place. This is where I see the Song of Songs serving so well. Like the holy of holies, it takes us behind the curtain to experience the intimate presence of Christ. We need to begin with Christ's spousal love for his bride. When we get that, when we know that, then we see our masculinity and femininity expressing this order of love and beckoning the beloved to Mount Zion.

Our chapters are beginning to culminate here, as I am now expanding on some points I introduced earlier. I mentioned in chapter 2 how the Song is Deuteronomic—the enactment and embodiment of the great command, "Love the LORD your God with all your heart, with all your soul, and with all your strength" (Deut. 6:5). And in it we see why that is our ultimate longing, desire, and fulfillment—because he first loved us.

The spousal love of God for his people is proclaimed throughout Scripture; we see it right in the beginning. It is expressed in his covenant with us. God wants us to know this, so he reminds his people over and over. And they sometimes get it and say it back to God:

> "I will confirm my covenant that is between me and you and your future offspring throughout their generations. It is a permanent covenant to be your God and the God of your offspring after you." (Gen. 17:7)

> "I will take you as my people, and I will be your God." (Ex. 6:7)

> "I will walk among you and be your God, and you will be my people." (Lev. 26:12)

> "You established your people Israel to be your own people forever, and you, LORD, have become their God." (2 Sam. 7:24)

"You will live in the land that I gave your ancestors; you will be my people, and I will be your God." (Ezek. 36:28)

"My dwelling place will be with them; I will be their God, and they will be my people." (Ezek. 37:27)

When Paul addressed the issues of his day, he began with this covenant love:

And what agreement does the temple of God have with idols? For we are the temple of the living God, as God said:

> I will dwell
> and walk among them,
> and I will be their God,
> and they will be my people. (2 Cor. 6:16)

We see its consummation in Revelation, where we've been meditating:

I also saw the holy city, the new Jerusalem, coming down out of heaven from God, prepared like a bride adorned for her husband.
Then I heard a loud voice from the throne: Look, God's dwelling is with humanity, and he will live with them. They will be his peoples, and God himself will be with them and will be their God. (21:2–3)

And there it is—this covenant with his people is spousal. We see that throughout Scripture as well.

> I will take you to be my wife forever.
> I will take you to be my wife in righteousness,

justice, love, and compassion.
I will take you to be my wife in faithfulness,
and you will know the LORD. (Hos. 2:19–20)

"Then I passed by you and saw you, and you were indeed
at the age for love. So I spread the edge of my garment
over you and covered your nakedness. I pledged myself
to you, entered into a covenant with you—this is the
declaration of the Lord GOD—and you became mine."
(Ezek. 16:8)

"Indeed, your husband is your Maker—
his name is the LORD of Armies—
and the Holy One of Israel is your Redeemer;
he is called the God of the whole earth." (Isa. 54:5)

For as a young man marries a young woman,
so your sons will marry you;
and as a groom rejoices over his bride,
so your God will rejoice over you. (Isa. 62:5)

Paul spoke of this spousal love in Ephesians 5:32: "This
mystery is profound, but I am talking about Christ and the
church," revealing that marriage is a picture of this very love of
Christ for his church! And so Paul could also say, "I am jealous
for you with a godly jealousy, because I have promised you in
marriage to one husband—to present a pure virgin to Christ"
(2 Cor. 11:2).

The Song of Songs enfleshes this covenant love. The bride
gets it. She gets what all of Scripture is about. And she can't
contain herself, bursting on the scene, saying, "Oh, that he
would kiss me with the kisses of his mouth!" (1:2). This line
is spoken to *us*. She wants us to hear. She is evangelical.

And throughout the Song, she sings of this spousal, covenantal love of God:

> My love is mine and I am his;
> he feeds among the lilies. (Song 2:16)

> I am my love's and my love is mine,
> he feeds among the lilies. (Song 6:3)

> I am my love's,
> and his desire is for me. (Song 7:10)

She, the bride/church, is the lilies. "Like a lily among thorns, so is my darling among the young women" (Song 2:2). This is not only desire redeemed. This is the eschatological aim of desire. This is it! The real deal! The true orientation of desire that is from Christ, through him, and to him (Rom. 11:36).

This is what we must first know. God desires his bride. Get in on that, and then we will have the orientation to talk about all these other issues of our day. This order of love is vital. And as I've previously written, it transforms the way we see ourselves and others. It transforms the way we view our masculinity and femininity. It transforms the way we think about our bodies. It transforms the way we think about life and sex.

We need to get behind the curtain and into the holy of holies. Like the bride in the Song, like Anna the prophetess, like the woman at the well, like Mary Magdalene, like the bride in Revelation, we receive and wear this love, calling others to it because we cannot contain an overflowing river.

Instead of responding to the so-called sexual revolution of the world and letting our culture set the categories of desire, the church needs to open her eyes to the true sexual reformation in God's Word.

THE MAN'S RULE OVER THE WOMAN

Anna Anderson claimed that how we interpret Genesis 3:16c will inform the way we view every other woman who shows up in the Bible, right down to the bride of Revelation. Not only that, but it will inform the way we view women now: the women in our homes, in our neighborhoods, in our workplaces, in our social circles, and in our churches. If her desire is a lust for power over the man that must be ruled over, then woman is a threat. She's someone to be suspicious of when she speaks and acts. Women are not to be trusted. They must be managed. As Diane Langberg says, "Much has been said throughout the centuries about what it means to be female. Men have said most of it."[54] This begs the question: do we view women the way the Son of man, Jesus, does?

What if this desire of the woman is a sign for us all—something that we are to cultivate as we come to know our Groom's desire for us? How does that change things? How does it change the way we think about desire? How does it change the way we think about our own desires and how they should be oriented? How does it change the way we think of ourselves as collectively desired by God as his exclusive people/bride? How do you think of your own body, then? How does it change the way you love others?

Hopefully we are all wanting to sing along with this wonderful news of God's spousal love for his bride. But where does that leave the ruling man of Genesis 3:16? I shared a few different interpretations. Is it a benevolent description of man as a refuge for the woman, a command that the man must assert his headship over the woman, or a description of brokenness

---

54. Diane Langberg, *Redeeming Power: Understanding Authority and Abuse in the Church* (Grand Rapids: Brazos, 2020), 95.

after the fall, describing a hierarchal patriarchy that is to follow and must be redeemed?[55]

I see plausibility in the first and last options but lean heavier on the latter. First, let's talk about that middle option that Foh championed. Since I do not find her interpretation of *teshuqah* a faithful rendering of the text, it affects the second clause in the sentence, "yet he will rule over you." Plus, the text is descriptive, not prescriptive. Furthermore, reading Genesis 3:16 in light of Paul's address to wives and husbands in Ephesians 5:22–33 contradicts this interpretation. I will get more into the latter argument in the following chapter—husbands are not told to rule over their wives but to love them.

The plausibility that I find in the first option, that this is a benevolent description, is how it should point us to our true King and spiritual head, Jesus Christ. As shown above, in the Song we see the bride taking refuge in her Groom. Likewise, husbands should desire to be the first spouse to serve in being a refuge. In the covenant formula we just followed through Scripture, we see God is our true God and we are his people. We certainly equate rulership with God. And we see how benevolent he is in these verses. So if we see these verses as showing a picture of God's rule over his bride, and husbands modeling that, we would have to check ourselves when it comes to what this rule means. In the Song, we may insinuate rule from the Groom's titles of king and shepherd, but it is expressed in action as a tender desire and love for his bride.

And that is why, while maybe conceding to a double meaning here, I agree with Anderson that Genesis 3:16 and 17 can be compared to show that just as man's good labor is now painful,

---

55. There is another proposed interpretation, by John Schmitt, that mšl in Gen. 3:16 should be translated "and he will be like you" (in having a mutual desire) rather than "he will rule over you." See John J. Schmitt, "Like Eve, Like Adam: mšl in Gen 3,16," *BIB* 72 (1991): 1-22.

the woman's good desire is now thwarted or unrequited. Male dominance plays a leading role in this. His rule. This is the story that we see unfolding in Scripture and even still today. And so immediately following Genesis 3 there are three vignettes of male violence. Matthew Lynch sums these up, revealing the beginning of "male warrior-rulers rul[ing] by conquering nature and conquering women":[56]

1. The beginning of polygamy (domestic verbal violence): Lamech, the first polygamist tried to outdo God by exacting unjust vengeance and then taunting his wives. [Gen 4:19–24]
2. The beginning of the warrior kings (military violence): Divine beings seized women and, surprise, surprise, their sons became warriors. [Gen. 6:1–5][57]
3. The beginning of "great" cities (political and civic violence): One warrior named Nimrod was the first warrior-hunter, the "ideal (royal) male" in the ancient world. He founded the great Mesopotamian cities. [Gen. 10][58]

The first ten chapters of the first book of the Bible reveal "the striking link between male domination and violence"[59] that we see throughout the rest of the Old Testament and even in our lives now. That is pretty sobering. We can't testify to a benevolent male rule throughout history that is a refuge to women. In that way, I see Genesis 3:16d as descriptive and prophetic. It's telling us why things are the way they are. It is not

---

56. Matthew J. Lynch, "The Roots of Violence: Male Violence against Women in Genesis," *The Biblical Mind* (blog), Center for Hebraic Thought, September 29, 2020, https://hebraicthought.org/male-violence-against-women-in-genesis/.

57. Lynch, "Roots of Violence," also notes the similar language in the fall account, replicating original sin: The divine beings *saw* (*rʾh*) that they were *pleasing* (*ṭôb*), so they *took* (*lqḥ*) as wives *from* (*min*) any whom they wanted (Gen 6:2).

58. Lynch, "Roots of Violence."

59. Lynch, "Roots of Violence."

telling us that all men are violent, but that male dominance and violence as the result of sin would be a key factor in thwarting the woman's desire.[60]

SING WITH ME

Jesus tells his disciples something quite different about what it means to rule, different from the world's view, and different from many in the church's view even today. It was radically different from what the disciples thought. He said, "You know that the rulers of the Gentiles lord it over them, and those in high positions act as tyrants over them. It must not be like that among you. On the contrary, whoever wants to become great among you must be your servant, and whoever wants to be first among you must be your slave, just as the Son of Man did not come to be served, but to serve, and to give his life as a ransom for many" (Matt. 20:25–28). This is worth singing about, right? Jesus is telling us that leadership is cruciform. That is, like Christ, it takes us to the cross in complete giving of ourselves for the sake of the beloved.

So is headship. Adam was a federal head of mankind. In this, he was a representative. If he obeyed God's parameters for creation, he would have earned eternal fellowship on the new heavens and the new earth with the triune God for all of us. His disobedience plunged mankind into the fall, bringing sure death and depravity on all his progeny. This depravity even affected the way he viewed his wife. Even as they still loved one another, their union was fractured. They could no longer be naked and unashamed. He threw her under the bus as soon as he was held accountable before God (Gen. 3:12).

---

60. We even see this in the Song's second night scene (Song 5:7).

The first woman has notoriously become a legalist in our Bible lessons about the fall. In speaking to the serpent about God's command, she added, "About the fruit of the tree in the middle of the garden, God said, 'You must not eat it *or touch it*, or you will die'" (Gen. 3:3, emphasis added). Was she really beginning to put fences around God's Word? After all, God himself didn't add "or touch it" when he gave this command to Adam (Gen. 2:17). Some say that maybe Adam added those words when conveying the command to Eve. Wayne Townsend suggests something different is going on here. Genesis is the first book of the Bible, giving us the origins of creation. But we need to keep its original, Levitical audience in mind. "Genesis was written to a redeemed people of God. Genesis, as received, contains an apologetic for the origins of Israel as a distinct nation and its claim on the land of Canaan. Thus, Genesis assumes the history of exodus-conquest, in the midst of which Israel received the law-code of Sinai."[61] Townsend notes how we see signs of the levirate marriage law code (Deut. 25:5–6) in the story of Judah and Tamar. Likewise, the account of the flood is told with an assumed prior knowledge of clean and unclean animals in relation to sacrifice. Genesis was written with its original audience already knowing and reading it "in the light of the law given at Sinai, including the cleanness code found in Leviticus."[62]

> In this context, the story of the Fall functions as a pretext for
> the exodus-conquest. Genesis 3 identifies the sources of evil
> that have led to the suffering of slavery. It also justifies the

---

61. P. Wayne Townsend, "Eve's Answer to the Serpent: An Alternative Paradigm for Sin and Some Implications in Theology," *CTJ* 33 (1998): 399–420, https://faculty .gordon.edu/hu/bi/ted_hildebrandt/otesources/01-genesis/text/articles-books / townsend_evesanswer_ctj.pdf.

62. Townsend, 403.

conquest by expanding the division between the woman and the Serpent to an ongoing struggle between their descendants (Gen. 3:15). All of this relies on a separation from, and over against, the rest of the nations—the very separation identified in the Levitical code (Lev.18:24–30; 20:22–27).[63]

This context sheds light on the woman's addition of "Do not touch." She is saying something prophetic here.

We find parallels to Eve's words in Leviticus 11 and Deuteronomy 14. Leviticus 11 defines food that is lawful for Israelites to eat. Concerning unclean land animals, verse 8 states, "You must not *eat* their meat or *touch* their carcasses; they are unclean for you" (emphasis added). The vocabulary and sentence structure of this verse strongly parallels Eve's words in Genesis 3:3: "You must not eat fruit . . . and you must not touch it."[64]

Original audiences would make this connection, as they knew the Levitical law. They knew that *touching* anything unclean would *make* Adam and Eve unclean. And the ramifications were fatal. They also knew that there must be a sacrifice at this point. Adam and Eve would be cast out of the sanctuary of the garden-temple. The woman was filling out the story with her extra words. And yet the serpent was able to deceive her, disorienting her desires. "The woman saw that the tree was good for food and delightful to look at, and that it was desirable for obtaining wisdom" (Gen. 3:6).

Do you see now how the suspense is building? We are at the edge of our seats! What will happen now? The scene is dripping

---

63. Townsend, 403.
64. Townsend, 406.

with uncleanliness and death. What will Adam do? He is the federal head. He represents mankind. He is the husband, united to his wife. Will he offer himself as the sacrifice?[65] Will he lay down his life for his wife? No. He doesn't point her to God as the source of all goodness and wisdom while there with her (Gen. 3:6), and he doesn't intervene on behalf of her after she partakes. Our federal head participates with her. Then he puts the blame on her.

While Adam failed in his headship and blamed his wife, Jesus Christ put the blame on himself to make his bride clean. He faced God's holy wrath against sin because sin is evil and it destroys the goodness God created. It makes us unclean, unfit to be in the presence of the pure and holy God. And it destroys us. He crushes Satan's head. The Son of God entered into his own creation, entered into our flesh, experienced our temptations without sinning, lived a righteous life before God on our behalf, laid aside his own rights to his divine power, and suffered outside the gate with the unclean. Why? To sanctify his bride by his blood (Heb. 13:12), making us holy and "cleansing [us] with the washing of water by the word" (Eph. 5:26). That's what a head is supposed to do. He sacrificially gives. That's what a groom is supposed to do. That's what masculinity is. Jesus doesn't look at us and see filthiness and death. He covers us. He sees his own likeness that he bestowed on us, and we hear his words to us in the procession of the bride: "You are absolutely beautiful, my darling; there is no imperfection in you" (Song 4:7).

And as this theme of uncleanliness, sin, and redemption plays out in Scripture, we are promised that we get to enter into that beauty. "Blessed are those who wash their robes, so that they may have the right to the tree of life and may enter

---

65. See L. Michael Morales, *Who Shall Ascend the Mountain of the Lord? A Biblical Theology of the Book of Leviticus*, NSBT (Downers Grove, IL: IVP, 2015), 181–84.

the city by the gates. Outside are the dogs, the sorcerers, the sexually immoral, the murderers, the idolaters, and everyone who loves and practices falsehood" (Rev. 22:14–15). The bride in Revelation is evangelically calling "the one who desires" to take the "water of life" (22:17). Doesn't that make you realize how thirsty you are?

Now, men, how can you possibly bear to look at pornography—to rob woman of her personhood so that you can consume her? For what? A desire that is so perverted from holy desire and can only destroy you and your victims. Men, you are to represent the true masculinity of our mutual head, Jesus Christ, who calls his bride "sister" first. He delights and invests in her holiness and purity.

Let's apply this truth to all our disoriented desires that we deceive ourselves into thinking will give us goodness. We try to disguise it or justify it because, as Christopher West says, we are full of shame. It's "a *failure to see the body as it truly is*: as a sign that points beyond itself to God. When this happens, our desire for Infinite Beauty (eros) gets 'stuck' on the body itself. The *icon* becomes an *idol*, and we come to worship the creature rather than the Creator. This is what Paul tells us in Romans 1, is what lust is."[66] It never satisfies because its whole orientation is diabolical. Perverted eros enslaves. West calls us to know true eros so that we can "reclaim what Satan has plagiarized."[67] Our disoriented desires are trying to steer us away from the spousal love of God. They deceive us into thinking that our bodies aren't meaningful, good, and signs of God's love.

West makes the remarkable claim that "the salvation of the world begins with the salvation of eros." Stop for a minute and just meditate on that. We see exactly this in the Song. That's

---

66. Christopher West, *Our Bodies Tell God's Story: Discovering the Divine Plan for Love, Sex, and Gender* (Grand Rapids: Brazos, 2020), 42, emphasis original.
67. West, 88.

why it's a song! Eros isn't to be a baser instinct; it is true love in action. And it undergirds how we view and treat one another. The eros love of God overflows, exclusively for his bride, and then it is modeled in her exclusive love for him, either in our singleness or in our exclusive marriages. Each status points to the eschatological eros with our Groom. And so West says, "And precisely because the relationship of man and woman is the deepest foundation of ethics and culture, when eros is misdirected, it leads to the 'whole moral disorder that deforms both sexual life and the functioning of *social, economic* and even cultural *life*.' Christ wants to save each human person and all of humanity at its roots, and *our roots are inextricably linked with eros.*"[68]

The first head of the human race failed. We see how the consequences revealed in the fall of an improper ruling, a counterfeit way of viewing woman, as well as a distorted way of viewing our bodies and our desires, has led to much destruction—both in Scripture and in our lives still today. What we need is to look to our true head, the head of the church/bride, Jesus Christ. In him, we see that, as Diane Langberg says, "Headship is cruciform; it goes by way of the cross."[69] We see that we are the desirous woman, "I am my love's and his desire is for me" (Song 7:10). We see redeeming eros that is overflowing.

---

68. West, 43, quoting from TOB 48:1, emphasis original.
69. Langberg, *Redeeming Power*, 102.

QUESTIONS FOR DISCUSSION

1. How does the way we think about desire affect our reading of Scripture and the way we relate to God?
2. How does it affect the dignity and personhood that we assign to men and women and the way that we love?
3. A prayer in *The Valley of Vision* ends with this request: "Fill the garden of my soul with the wind of love, that the scents of the Christian life may be wafted to others; then come and gather fruits to thy glory. So I shall fulfill the great end of my being—to glorify thee and be a blessing to men."[70] How could this prayer be an application to Song of Songs 4:16 and a response to God's desire?

70. Arthur Bennett, ed., "Things Needful," *The Valley of Vision: A Collection of Puritan Prayers & Devotions* (Carlisle, PA: Banner of Truth Trust, 1975), 325.

Chapter Five

SEXUALITY AS GIFT

We often describe masculinity and femininity as attributes that we are to put on. The Council on Biblical Manhood and Womanhood (CBMW) has taught us to talk about our sexuality in terms of "roles." Performing these roles is the answer to their call for "masculine males and feminine females."[1] As I covered in the first chapter, man's role is to lead the way in all decision-making and woman's role is to affirm and puff this male potency, because men are authoritative and women are submissive. If circumstances are dire in that the roles switch up for the woman—say, she earns more money than the man or is a single parent providing for and protecting her children—then she just needs to be careful to do this with a "uniquely feminine demeanor."[2] She would not want to overstep in these ways if the husband were in the picture though, as that would be "taking up the masculine calling."[3] This vision of sexuality being taught to the church is a fragile enterprise.

All this is curious to me, as CBMW seems to be fueling some of the very philosophies they want to combat. Isn't this the same kind of thinking perpetuated by the transgender

---

1. Ligon Duncan, preface to *Recovering Biblical Manhood and Womanhood*, ed. John Piper and Wayne Grudem (1991; repr., Wheaton, IL: Crossway, 2006), xii.

2. John Piper, "A Vision of Biblical Complementarity," in *Recovering Biblical Manhood and Womanhood*, ed. John Piper and Wayne Grudem (1991; repr., Wheaton, IL: Crossway, 2006), 37.

3. Piper, 37.

movement? Isn't the whole idea that men could be something other than men, or a woman needing a "uniquely feminine demeanor," the same mindset of the latest stage of the sexual revolution? Is there a biological part of me that has a uterus and makes me a woman that's different than my soul and psyche, which needs to make sure it *acts* like a woman? And what is it that I need to do as a woman to *be* more womanly? Why is being female not good enough, so that I need to figure out what it is to be a *feminine* female? And what *is* a uniquely feminine demeanor?

I agree with CBMW that there are distinctions and differences between men and women. I do not think, however, that we need to be stumbling about trying to hyper-focus on whether we are masculine or feminine *enough*. CBMW has capitalized on this kind of language, using the word *role*, which is a theater term meaning "playing a part," to refer to performed ontological differences between men and women. And as I've said, these differences are a polished version of Aristotelian notions. When we go back to the definitions provided by CBMW for "mature" masculinity and femininity, we see where they are going.[4] To be a woman, I must be a certain way, play a certain role, fit a certain cultural stereotype.[5] It's like there is some kind of imaginary scale of actualization to become a truly feminine female. Huldah, Deborah, Jael, Ruth, Dorcas, Phoebe, Priscilla, and Junia—just to name a few—must have missed the memo!

Again, we need to return to the metaphysical understanding that the body and soul exist in hylomorphic unity.[6] As Prudence Allen put it, we understand that as the image of God there are "two distinct ways of being a human being, as a male and as a

---

4. See p. 1.
5. See Piper, "A Vision," 41, 50–51.
6. See Prudence Allen, *The Concept of Woman*, vol. 3, *The Search for Communion of Persons, 1500–2015* (Grand Rapids: Eerdmans, 2016), 492. This contrasts with Plato's dualistic view of the body and soul.

female."[7] I think CBMW agrees with this, but their language and teaching on manhood and womanhood betrays them. There aren't half men, clueless as to how to earn their man card. There aren't biologically identifiable women with masculine souls. We don't need to force our sexual distinctions under an artificial ontological framework of authority and submission or other cultural stereotypes. I don't have to act like a woman to be actualized—I am a woman in all my actions. We don't need "masculine males" and "feminine females." We need to recognize our sexuality as gift. The language CBMW uses leads to the conclusions we hear in the transgender community, such as "I am a woman trapped in a man's body." God has already created us as men and women, and he has also created us as unique persons. Let's talk about the meaningfulness of that.

This way of thinking makes me very cautious about what language is being used by organizations such as CBMW to lead the way in talking about the serious issues the church needs to address regarding sexuality. After all, we are talking about real people, not just economy and ethics. With the proper metaphysical understanding of the hylomorphic unity of the body and soul, we can minister to those who are suffering with gender dysphoria rather than rubbing salt in their wounds. We aren't actualized as men and women by a role we play or by a "feeling" of femininity. And broken, hurting people are still whole people who need encouragement in the gospel about the spousal love of God—for their souls and their bodies together. If we are washed clean by the blood of the Lamb, he says to us, "You are absolutely beautiful, my darling; there is no imperfection in you" (Song 4:7). These words have an already-and-not-yet meaning. We know that the bodies we now have, that are

---

7. Allen, 3:464. Allen recognizes that most of us are male or female, but because of the fall, a small percentage of people, who should receive equal dignity, suffer with intersex biology.

affected by sin and the fall, are not the same as the glorified bodies we will have on the new heavens and the new earth. It's understandable that not only the extreme cases of gender dysphoria but indeed all of us struggle to "fit into" and be satisfied in our bodies in this age. They groan with creation:

> For I consider that the sufferings of this present time are not worth comparing with the glory that is going to be revealed to us. For the creation eagerly waits with anticipation for God's sons to be revealed. For the creation was subjected to futility—not willingly, but because of him who subjected it—in the hope that the creation itself will also be set free from the bondage to decay into the glorious freedom of God's children. For we know that the whole creation has been groaning together with labor pains until now. Not only that, but we ourselves who have the Spirit as the firstfruits—we also groan within ourselves, eagerly waiting for adoption, the redemption of our bodies. (Rom. 8:18–23)

Our groaning is appropriate. And notice that not only will that great day be the day of our consummation as the bride of Christ, as we have been seeing throughout Scripture, but also of our adoption as sons in the Son.[8] While men and women have a joint telos, women can learn from men what it means to be sons in the Son, and men can learn from women more about what it means to be the bride of Christ. Additionally, in the first man and woman we see a representation of the anticipated union of earth (man, as from the dust) and heaven (woman, as not from the dust).[9] If we miss these representations, we easily fall off

---

8. See David B. Garner, *Sons in the Son: The Riches and Reach of Adoption in Christ* (Phillipsburg, NJ: P&R, 2016).

9. Thanks to Anna Anderson for helping me further develop this representation of heaven and earth; personal communication.

the rails into legalism, conflating description and prescription, and policing cultural ethics. We must be more careful. In all this, our eyes need to be on Christ as we move toward a holy communion of persons, fostering a mutual knowledge of one another that results in dynamic, fruitful reciprocity through the giving of ourselves in and through our differences.[10]

NEIGHBORING SEXES

When we use cultural stereotypes or roles as essential elements of femininity and masculinity, we are reducing our brothers and sisters and missing out on God's creative design of human beings as unique, unrepeatable people. Dorothy Sayers suggested that men and women are not opposite sexes but neighboring sexes.[11] This doesn't diminish the distinctions between men and women but rather recognizes that both men and women are human. Understanding this basic fact helps us see the holistic beauty of God's design and opens the doors for men and women to serve one another by giving of themselves as complete whole people in synergetic[12] and dynamic fellowship.

Prudence Allen breaks down "four demonstratable principles: equal dignity, significant difference, synergetic relation, and intergenerational fruition."[13] Allen says that it's all right there in Genesis:

The principle of *equal dignity* of all human beings is revealed in Genesis 1:26, "Let us make man [the human being] in our

---

10. See Allen, *Concept of Woman*, 3:460.

11. Dorothy Sayers, "The Human-Not-Quite-Human," in *Are Women Human? Astute and Witty Essays on the Role of Women in Society* (1971; repr., Grand Rapids: Eerdmans, 2005), 53.

12. Cooperative.

13. Allen, *Concept of Woman*, 3:493.

image, after our likeness." The *significant difference* between woman and man is revealed in 1:27: "in the image of God he created them; male and female he created them." The *synergetic relation* of a woman and man is revealed in 1:28: "And God blessed them, and God said to them, 'be fruitful and multiply,'" and in 2:24: "they became one flesh." The fourth principle of *intergenerational fruition* is revealed in 5:1–32: "This is the book of the generations," and in the subsequent listing of those who generated one generation after another from Adam to Noah.[14]

These principles show forth in marriage but also in platonic, chaste friendships and partnerships in our neighborhoods, churches, work, and other communities. Our shared dignity and significant differences compel us to communion and to giving out of these differences, ultimately moving us to the greatest fruition of all, a communion of saints in union with our Groom.

MAN WITHOUT DIGNITY AND PERSONHOOD

This language of "feminine females" and "masculine males" can become very confusing and unhelpful. It moves us to focus on basing our sexuality on prescriptive cultural mores. And it doesn't recognize our *given* sexuality for its own value. This hurts the dignity and personhood of both men and women. I want to acknowledge the real struggle men have to measure up to this extrabiblical category of the masculine man. It can start when they are young. Little boys are teased for being too

---

14. Allen, 3:494, emphasis original.

sensitive. Not assertive enough. Too soft. Their parents may grow overly concerned because they don't like the so-called manly stuff like sports and hunting. They might not be interested in the young men's youth group activities like whitewater rafting and ax throwing. Some of these boys grow up thinking maybe they aren't masculine enough. Their masculinity isn't seen as a gift to others. They struggle with gender security. Some, as a result, struggle with gender identity. To reduce manhood to these specific cultural qualities that need to be "put on," is to assault the dignity and personhood of each male who reflects the image of God in his body, personality, interests, and relationships with other persons. Jesus Christ, a man, wouldn't fare well here. He depended on women to support his ministry (Luke 8:1–3). He cried (John 11:35). He compared himself to a hen gathering her chicks under her wings in the way he wanted to gather Jerusalem's children together (Matt. 23:37).[15]

Dr. Joaquín Navarro-Valls, in his second briefing on the Holy See's position regarding the Fourth World Conference on Women, put it well: "Women and men are the illustration of a biological, individual, personal, and spiritual complementarity. Femininity is the unique and specific characteristic of woman, as masculinity is of man."[16] Men don't need to act a certain way to affirm their masculinity. Their actions are masculine

---

15. On the other hand, we do see in culture men and women who purposefully try to "put on" so-called masculine or feminine traits of the neighboring sex. I agree that this is troubling. When men "put on" feminine stereotypes of our culture in their mannerisms, interests, and sometimes the way they dress, they are putting on an artificial identity. This behavior grossly misunderstands the essence of the female and the concept of woman. It is an offense to womanhood. It robs both sexes of their dignity and personhood. Mimicking cultural stereotypes is not an expression of individuality or sexual identity. Trying to take on another's persona—especially as a misrepresentation of the other—is not an expression of self-worth. Furthermore, men are called to sacrificially love women, not try to become them.

16. Joaquin Navarro-Valls, "To Promote Woman's Equal Dignity," Priests for Life, August 25, 1995, https://www.priestsforlife.org/magisterium/navarrobeijing 08-25-95.htm.

because they are men. Let's not get that backward or we really offend personhood. It perverts the real, organic connection between our ontology as man or woman and how the gift of our sexuality is represented in life. This isn't based on cultural mores but on how our given distinctions represent unitive love.

It enhances the dignity of man to affirm the value of the unique person God has created him to be, over and against a faux, mask-wearing masculinity of the culture. Let's take off the masks: Stoicism is not true self-control. Aggression is not the same as courage. Dominance is not leadership. Violence is not the same as righteous anger. These masks are weak and impotent. And the positive qualities encouraged here are not only masculine qualities.

Furthermore, compassionate men are not effeminate. Men who commit their way to the Lord are not effeminate. Humble men are not effeminate. Men who exercise meekness are not effeminate. They are strong. They are a gift, helping to glorify the name of our Savior and to promote the goodness of their neighbor—dynamic and fructifying acts. Both men and women are to look to Jesus for Christian virtue. We are not directed to masculine manhood or feminine womanhood. We are not even directed to biblical manhood or biblical womanhood. We are men and women who are together directed to Christ, who called both men and women blessed who were poor in Spirit, mourners, gentle, thirsting for righteousness, merciful, pure in heart, peacemakers, and persecuted for his sake (Matt. 5:1–10).

A GIFT ACCEPTED OR REJECTED

Even though I have some significant differences with Roman Catholic doctrine, and therefore with some of Pope John Paul

II's premises, his *Theology of the Body*[17] is still a breath of fresh air from what is being taught about men and women in many Protestant circles, because he highlighted personhood and gift.[18] Pope John Paul II described our two different ways of being human, male and female, as the gift of our sexual bodies that pictures Christ's spousal love for his church. Or as Christopher West describes it, "God's plan of love stamped in [our] sexuality."[19] Now here is a gospel story! This word *gift* reveals so much. It reveals God's incredible generosity. It even tells us something about authority, which I will get to. The word *gift* also shines a light to reveal our own gratitude, or lack thereof. Do we see our sexuality as a gift? Do we see the sexuality of our brothers and sisters as a gift? How does that change the way we view ourselves and others? How does that change the way we treat others?

We live in a pornographic culture where sexuality is reduced and marketed for consumption. The pornographic culture wants sex minus the person. It denies dignity and personhood. Christians know that is not the intent of our sexuality. While the biblical manhood and womanhood (BMW) movement rejects this pornographic culture, its theology of man and woman falls into this same denial of personhood. Our sexuality is reduced to performance of roles and hierarchical structures without reciprocal enrichment. Let me explain.

Our posture of gratitude reveals something about what we think about the Giver. Our response to the gift reveals whether we think the Giver is good, what goodness is, where it comes

---

17. John Paul II, *Man and Woman He Created Them: A Theology of the Body*, trans. Michael Waldstein (Boston: Pauline Books & Media, 1986, 2006).

18. Aside from some of the more obvious doctrines that contrast with Protestant theology, I'd also include his teaching on the "divinization" of the body and "participation" in the eternal life of God.

19. Christopher West, *Our Bodies Tell God's Story: Discovering the Divine Plan for Love, Sex, and Gender* (Grand Rapids: Brazos, 2020), 53.

from, and what we should do with it. How do we honor God with the gift of our sexuality? How do we honor others? Here's something to consider that can be revealing: Is our gratitude something we practice within a community in response to our gratitude for God, or is it more of an individualistic means to experience our own personal fullness?

Christine Pohl elaborates: "Centuries ago, Seneca wisely warned that 'one should never accept a gift if one would be ashamed to acknowledge the debt publicly (Ben 2.23.1); a gift should be accepted only if the recipient is willing to 'invite the whole city to witness it.'"[20] How might this relate to our sexuality? How do we view the gift God has given us as man and as woman? Do we view others as gifts from God? And what does this gift then authorize us to do? Our gratitude should shape how we orient our desires in love and how we receive the gifts of male and female personhood at home, in the church, and in society. As we desire God, we will see others and want to love them the way he does.

RECIPROCAL ENRICHMENT

The creation account should provoke a sense of gratitude in recognizing the gift of sexual difference. John Paul II started with creation itself as a gift of God's Love (he capitalized this Love).[21] In the beginning, man was given this gift of life in the created world, but he was in solitude and saw there was no other like him. There was no community for him to practice gratitude in reciprocity. And in his solitude, man was unable to fully know

---

20. Christine D. Pohl, *Living into Community: Cultivating Practices That Sustain Us* (Grand Rapids: Eerdmans, 2012), 40.

21. John Paul II, *Man and Woman*, TOB 14:4, 183.

himself as a person because there was no other "I" before him. Personhood necessitates relationship. In God's declaration that it was not good for man to be alone, and that he would make a helper for him (Gen. 2:18), Pope John Paul II saw "alone" and "help" as key for man and woman to experience the essence of the gift of humanity as image of God. Woman helps man to recognize his own humanity and to gain a consciousness of reciprocal enrichment and the unitive meaning of the body in its masculinity and femininity.[22] So not only is she a gift, but she enables him to see himself as a gift.

> In fact, the gift reveals, so to speak, *a particular characteristic of human existence*, or even the very essence of the person. When God-Yahweh says, "It is not good that man should be alone" (Gen 2:18), he affirms that, "alone," the man does not completely realize this essence. He realizes that it is only by existing *"with someone"*—and, put even more deeply and completely, by existing *"for someone"* . . . communion of persons means living in a reciprocal "for," in a relationship of reciprocal gift. And this relationship is precisely the fulfillment of "man's" original solitude.[23]

Adam's singing proclamation reveals this. "When the 'male' man, awakened from his Genesis sleep, says, 'This time she is flesh from my flesh and bone from my bones' (Gen 2:23), these words in some way express the subjectively beautifying beginning of man's existence in the world."[24] Pope John Paul II continued, saying that man was conveying in this proclamation, *"Look, a body that expresses the 'person'!* . . . One can also say that

---

22. John Paul II, *Man and Woman*, TOB 9:5; 10:2; and 12:3, 165, 167, 175.
23. John Paul II, *Man and Woman*, TOB 14:2, 182, emphasis original.
24. John Paul II, *Man and Woman*, TOB 14:3, 182.

this 'body' reveals the 'living soul,' which man became when God (Yahweh) breathed life into him (see Gen. 2:7)."[25]

Man(kind) moved through the depth of original solitude, where he had no corresponding strength to help him identify his own personhood. He then emerged not only to understand himself but to a whole new "dimension of reciprocal gift, the expression of which—by that very fact the expression of his existence as a person—is the human body in all the original truth of its masculinity and femininity. The body, which expresses femininity 'for' masculinity and vice versa, masculinity 'for' femininity, manifests the reciprocity and the communion of persons."[26] We image divine love as mutual gifts to each other through our masculinity and femininity. In this way, our bodies are linked to the way we participate in the visible world.[27] They manifest us as man or woman,[28] as we communicate God's Word, radiate his love, and share that in communion with one another.

POWER TO EXPRESS LOVE

Our sexuate installation as man and woman manifests the spousal meaning of the body. We see this in what happens right after Adam's proclamation—they were naked and unashamed (Gen. 2:25). Our bodies, our sexuality, are gift, given by God, with "the power to express love: precisely that love in which the human person becomes a gift and—through this gift— fulfills the very meaning of his being and existence. . . . Man cannot 'fully find himself except through a sincere gift of self'

---

25. John Paul II, *Man and Woman*, TOB 14:4, 183, emphasis original.
26. John Paul II, *Man and Woman*, TOB 14:4, 183.
27. John Paul II, *Man and Woman*, TOB 12:3, 175.
28. John Paul II, *Man and Woman*, TOB 12:5, 176.

[*Gaudium et Spes*, 24:3]."[29] Pope John Paul II continued, "The human body, oriented from within by the 'sincere gift' of the person . . . reveals not only its masculinity or femininity on the physical level, but also reveals such a value and such a beauty that it goes beyond the simply physical level of 'sexuality.'" He explained that when we welcome this gift, it affirms the value of the other as a unique and unrepeatable person. "The 'affirmation of the person' is nothing other than welcoming the gift, which, through reciprocity, creates the communion of persons."[30] This is both an external expression of the body as well as an internal intimacy and knowing.

In marriage we see the great mystery of Christ's spousal love for his church. I've written about how our sexual distinctions as male and female represent this order of love. But our sexuality as gift goes beyond erotic one-flesh love in marriage. Recognizing others as gift orients the way that we love and the way we exercise our responsibilities in our relationships and communities as receivers.

WOMAN WITHOUT DIGNITY AND PERSONHOOD

Now let's go back to the subordinate ontology of woman and male ontological authority still taught in many factions of the church. This unbiblical ontological view among many in the biblical manhood and womanhood movement is a rejection of the feminine gift and a rejection of the personhood of women. Our bodies are theological. They are visible signs that tell us something about our God.

---

29. John Paul II, *Man and Woman*, TOB 15:1, 185–86.
30. John Paul II, *Man and Woman*, TOB 15:4, 188.

So God created man
in his own image;
he created him in the image of God;
he created them male and female. (Gen. 1:27)

Many teachers in the BMW movement want to tell us that the theology our bodies teach is that men are in authority over women. Somehow this is complementary. That's the story. The gospel story. If you challenge that, you are a feminist. Their very definition of "mature femininity"—where woman's femininity is measured by how she affirms, receives, and nurtures strength and leadership from worthy men—does not delineate woman as gift. Rather, she is parasitic to male authority. It's the other side of the same coin of how the porn culture views women. She has no dignity of personhood in the definition. BMW's ontology of male authority and female subordination rejects the feminine gift. Where is there room for her freedom here? How can there be a free, sincere gift of self when there is no self? And when there is no agency to give it? Where is her dignity and uniqueness of personhood? You cannot receive from woman if you do not *see* the gift.

There is no welcoming of woman's gift if she cannot ever give direct or personal guidance. No reciprocity. No dynamism. No true communion of persons. As Virginia Woolf put it, "Women have served all these centuries as looking-glasses possessing the magic and delicious power of reflecting the figure of man twice its natural size."[31] And this philosophy shows up all over the place in the teaching that is saturating our churches. Femininity is not seen as a gift but as a threat that needs to be managed. Woman's "role" is to inflate the man. Follow his decisions. A pastor and author in the BMW movement once told

31. Virginia Woolf, *A Room of One's Own* (New York: Harvest, 1989), 35.

me that woman is auxiliary to the man. Translation: She's to hold the looking glass for the man while taking care his domestic needs are met. A "feminine female" has to turn off what is unique to her as a person. She can't freely give of her *self*.

BMW talks much about male authority and female submission to it. And their usage of the word *authority*[32] denies the feminine gift. Yes, when you receive a gift, that authorizes you. It's not his ontology that gives man authority, it is his receiving the gifts of creation and of woman. What is man authorized to do? He is authorized to sacrifice his very body in loving her. He is authorized to welcome her—first and last as sister. His authorization is not to tell her what to do or to rule over her. That robs her dignity. That is a description of the fall. And it is evidenced in Adam's response to God, "The woman you gave to be with me. . . ." Listen to that ingratitude! *What did you give me, God? My gift is defective!*

BMW teaches the opposite of Adam's first expression toward woman (Gen. 2:23), which is echoed by the Bridegroom of the Song of Songs: "You have captured my heart, my sister, my bride. You have captured my heart with one glance of your eyes" (4:9). When Adam saw woman for the first time, he saw the eschatological beauty of the telos of man and woman, the union of heaven and earth, the union of Christ with his bride, and the communion of the saints. As God gives man woman, and woman man, they are both authorized to love and promote the holiness of the other in their aim for eternal communion with God and his people. And man, created first, is authorized to be the first to love, the first to sacrifice, the first to serve, the first to give power *to* other persons, not to exercise power

---

32. See John Piper and Wayne Grudem, *50 Crucial Questions: An Overview of Central Concerns about Manhood and Womanhood* (Wheaton, IL: Crossway, 1992, 2016), q. 36., p. 56; see https://document.desiringgod.org/50-crucial-questions-about-manhood-and-womanhood-en.pdf?ts=1471551126.

over them. We see this distortion of the gift as the effects of the fall, described in Genesis 3:16. But the bride's response in the Song of Songs reveals desire restored in Christ as we saw in chapter 4, "I am my love's, and his desire is for me" (Song 7:10). That is true freedom in belonging. That is the story we tell as men and women.

JOY IN RECEIVING THE GIFT

Our bodies, our whole selves as men and women, tell the story of the great joy with which Christ received the gift of his bride, the church. He is bringing her to the holy of holies, having taken on flesh and penetrated behind the veil, securing communion with his bridal people in sacred space. He gave himself as the ultimate gift, and he loves us to the end.

Our bodies tell the story of the power to love. Pope John Paul II described love itself as a power—to share, by the Holy Spirit, in rejoicing in the truth and in the value of God's creation and redemption.[33] Christ, our true gift, rejoices in his bride. And she rejoices in him. Does the church make this story visible to the watching world? Or do we contradict ourselves when we uphold distinction between the sexes and yet reject the feminine gift? The bride signifies the eternal complement[34]

---

33. See John Paul II, *Man and Woman*, TOB 15:1, 185–86.

34. I am borrowing the description "eternal complement" from Anna Anderson; personal correspondence. I see this as another way of affirming the doctrine of *totus Christus*, that is, the "total Christ"—Christ and his church. Herman Bavinck described, "The pleroma (fullness) that dwells in Christ must also dwell in the church. It is being filled with all the fullness of God (Eph. 3:19; Col. 2:2, 10). It is God whose fullness fills Christ (Col. 1:19), and it is Christ whose fullness in turn fills the church (Eph. 1:23). . . . As the church does not exist apart from Christ, so Christ does not exist without the church. . . . Together with him it can be called the one Christ (1 Cor. 12:12)." In Herman Bavinck, *Reformed Dogmatics*, vol. 3, *Sin and Salvation in Christ*, ed. John Bolt, trans. John Vriend (Grand Rapids: Baker Academic, 2006), 474.

to the Son and the Father's great love for the Son in the gift that he gave him.

How we treat our women reveals our eschatological anticipation of joy. The bride is a gift. And sisters are a gift. Like Christ for his sister, his bride, women in the church should be invested with power *to*—power to experience freedom in belonging; power to wear, fructify, and return Christ's love; power to be a corresponding strength for their brothers. Does the church publicly welcome this gift, or are their women looked at as subjects to fulfill individual men's concupiscence, promote their masculinity, and follow their "loving" orders? What does our affirmation of the gift of femininity look like?

God's whole design of men and women is evangelical. That is, we are sharers of the *euangelion*, the good news. And Christ says to his bride, "Companions are listening for your voice; let me hear you!" (Song 8:13). Rejecting the feminine gift is actually a rejection of the authority of God, the Gift Giver. Giving is an act of authority. And in God's act of giving, the receiver is authorized to reciprocally give love.

WHAT'S THIS ABOUT POWER
TO VERSUS POWER *OVER*?

I want to focus a little more on this distinction I made between giving power to other persons and exercising power over them. I was listening to a fascinating discussion about power and trust on a secular podcast called *Work Life with Adam Grant*, between organizational psychologist Adam Grant and clinical psychologist Esther Perel.[35] It made me think a lot about all

---

35. Adam Grant and Esther Perel, *Work Life with Adam Grant*, March 2020, https://www.ted.com/talks/worklife _with_adam_grant_bonus_relationships

the discussions around authority and submission. Here is an excerpt, with a few edits, of what Esther Perel said about power:

> There is no relationship that doesn't have a power dimension. It's intrinsic to relationships. It's not good or bad, just part of the fabric of relationships. Because in relationships you have expectations, and with expectations comes a degree of dependency/reliance, and that dependency is conferred to the people on whom you depend . . . [bestowing] power. And that power gets neutralized by making it become something that is benevolent, which we then call "trust." So that it will become power *to* rather than power *over*. But everybody understands that power is not just a vertical axis that comes with authority. Anybody who's had a two-year-old knows that. . . . You can have power that comes from the bottom up, the power that constantly deflects energy, the power that takes the authority away from the people in authority. Power is multifaceted.[36]

She continued, saying that we need to be asking questions about the dynamic of power in a relationship to see if it is healthy: "Is this power helping the system drive—doing what it needs to do in the relationship? Or is this power that becomes oppressive, abused, which means a breach of trust?"[37]

It made me think of the context of Paul's letter to the Ephesians. He was speaking in a patriarchal society where the *paterfamilias*, the property owner who ruled the household, had power *over*. Working from the main imperative that the address to wives, children, slaves, and husbands came from, "Don't get

---

_at_work_with_esther_perel?language=en&referrer=playlist-worklife_with_adam _grant_season_3.

36. Grant and Perel, *Work Life with Adam Grant*.
37. Grant and Perel, *Work Life with Adam Grant*.

drunk with wine, which leads to reckless living, but be filled by the Spirit" (5:18), Paul detailed what it would look like to be filled by the Spirit in the Christian life and in our relationships. I'm going to skip over the way we speak to one another and get to the specific dynamic he addressed in submitting to one another. I want to start with the one who has power *over* in the household, whom Paul addressed the most in this text. And I am only going to be addressing the husband-wife relationship in the text. Paul did not tell the husband to rule his wife, which was the cultural way of life at the time (and the description after the fall), but said something quite radical instead—*love her.*

And what he described in these verses is a love that gives power *to.* It is a love that sacrifices the husband's own rights, his own prestige, his own body, to elevate and serve his wife. Paul reveals the great mystery that is unlocked in the Song of Songs—marriage is a symbol of Christ's love for his bride, the church. So as I quoted from Pope John Paul II before, "The symbol of the Bridegroom is masculine."[38] And yet husbands cannot do all that Christ has done for his bride. Paul even alluded to this in his letter when he said that "Christ loved the church and gave himself for her to make her holy, cleansing her with the washing of water by the Word. He did this to present the church to himself in splendor, without spot or wrinkle or anything like that, but holy and blameless" (Eph. 5:25–27).

If you are a singer of the Song, you will recognize that language. After praising seven parts of the bride's body in a *wasf* when she is presented to him, using the very language of sacred space to describe her, we hear the Groom sing, "You are absolutely beautiful, my darling; there is no imperfection in you" (Song 4:7). No stain. No spot or wrinkle. Our husbands

---

38. John Paul II, *Mulieris Dignitatem*, apostolic letter, August 15, 1988, §25, http://www.vatican.va/content/john-paul-ii/en/apost_letters/1988/documents/hf_jp-ii_apl_19880815_mulieris-dignitatem.html.

don't have to make us holy, because Christ, our Bridegroom, has. But as men, as the bridegroom in the marriage, they are given the power to represent this kind of love. As Pope John Paul II said, the order of love should begin with the man. This is his submission. And when he looks to his wife, he should see the glory of what is to come, the eschatological beauty of the radiance that is our end in perfect communion with Christ and one another. By giving his wife power *to*—power to experience freedom in belonging; power to wear, fructify, and return that love; power to be a corresponding strength—he is even loving himself. She represents their eschatological glory of which we get a taste in the Song.

And practically speaking, this is how we build trust. The wife will know what she is in the relationship—loved and valued. Dignified. True voluntary submission wells out of trust. We defer to one another when we trust. This is what we want. This is true intimacy. Our sexuality is gift.

And yet Paul spoke to wives first. After calling Christians to be filled by the Spirit by submitting to one another, he called wives to submit to their husbands. It was radical for Paul even to address the wife in a household code like this. Usually the *paterfamilias* was the only one addressed in Greco-Roman culture, even though in reality wives were the domestic managers of the household.[39] Nevertheless, he began with the wives. Foremost, they were to submit to the Lord, the true Bridegroom. And let's not take this lightly. Because just as Perel noted, power can come from the bottom up. Power is a complex thing that has an interdependence of parts. It's not always what we think it is or even how we think we see it. Perel explains how she

---

39. See Carolyn Osiek and Margaret Y. MacDonald with Janet H. Tulloch, *A Woman's Place: House Churches in Earliest Christianity* (Minneapolis: Fortress, 2006), 154–63. Also, these authors discuss woman as *paterfamilias* when she is the head of the household.

learned more about this during a clinical case in a dynamic with a depressed person. The depressed person seemed inept and powerless, but the true dynamic was that the depressed person had all the power. "Through their impotence, they were actually activating the competence of everybody else who was trying to lift them, to whom they end up saying no to everything they suggest to them, and in the end the competent people feel as defeated and deflated as the depressed one. That is power."[40]

Wives, this means no power games for power *over* your husband, who is called to love you in a vulnerable way. Give him the power to do that in your submission to him. Don't sabotage him. Then he will trust you and treasure you, if he is a godly man. (If he is an abusive man, this doesn't apply, and vice versa.)

Instead of simplifying power, hold this complexity. See its beauty. Look to Christ, who, as described in these verses by Paul, gave his bride, the church, power *to*—to the greatest aim ever—experience holiness and freedom in belonging, and to love and be loved by God.

As my friend Anna Anderson, who has been a great conversation partner on hashing out all of this, put it,

> Woman as second represents the glorious second order. The goal of redeemed humanity is pictured in the prophets as domesticated and bucolic, feasting and reclining. We are gathered and nurtured by God, like a hen gathers her chicks. It is homecoming after war, where swords are beaten into plowshares. Yet what woman represents is descriptive, not prescriptive in this life. Deborah goes out to war, yet because she is a type of the second order, this is not normative. But she has not sinned.[41]

---

40. Grant and Perel, *Work Life with Adam Grant*.
41. Anna Anderson, personal communication, March 9, 2020.

Rather than reduce God's Word and say woman is created second because she is subordinate, we need to see the whole redemptive story God is telling here. Woman was created second from man's very side as his glory, meaning, when Adam saw Eve, he saw his telos as the bride of Christ, the church flowing out of Christ's wounded side. Anderson added,

> Woman images the peace and nurture of the eternal city. Man, the guardian and protector of sacred space, images Christ who defeats all of his and our enemies and takes his bride. And yet these are descriptive, not prescriptive categories. Ruth protects and provides for Naomi and takes her husband, Boaz. Paul is a nurturing mother, and Christ is mother (a picture of Yahweh in the OT), longing to gather her chicks. We cannot absolutize these as prescriptions and prohibitions.[42]

So we don't have to reduce Mary Magdalene's act as a mere witness. The Lord Jesus Christ authorized her to go be an apostle to the apostles, as she has been known throughout church history. We don't downplay the women Paul called coworkers, or the church planters, the prophets, or the ones who risked their necks for him. Like the picture we see in Romans 16, we can be thankful for men and women colaborers serving under the fruit of the ministry with reciprocal voices and dynamic exchange. Not all contributions in the church are hierarchies. When we read about disciples in the Bible, is it just talking to the men?[43] And how can the men in the church grow in the teleological[44] understanding of their humanness, as part of the collective

---

42. Anna Anderson, personal communication.
43. This question has been thrust before me as a woman writing about discipleship.
44. Meaning how their design as men is related to their end, or ultimate hope.

bride of Christ, if they cannot learn from or be influenced by women? The masculine gift isn't to micromanage. It's to love. It's for men to use their power to love. And men are not the only ones with power. Maybe that's why it is such a threat for some when women exercise direct or personal guidance over a man. They can't receive that. Why not?

SING WITH ME

It is by understanding our ontology, including our metaphysical body-soul hylomorphic unity as gift, that we can begin to understand our sexuality. Before the beginning of time, an intratrinitarian[45] covenant of redemption was made between the persons of the Godhead, whereby God the Father promised to give the Son a bride, the Son promised to secure the redemption of his bride, and the Holy Spirit promised to apply his work to his people. The bride is a gift given in eternity. This isn't arbitrary or based on any merits of the bride but is an election because of God's love (Eph. 2:4–5). The triune God loves us. Let that sink in. He calls us into eternal communion with himself.

The collective bride of Christ gets to know something of the outgoing, overflowing love of the triune God, as we are created to share covenantally in the Father's love for the Son, through the Holy Spirit. This is our end. Jesus alluded to this in the High Priestly Prayer when he said, "Father, I want those you have given me to be with me where I am, so that they will see my glory, which you have given me because you loved me before

---

45. An eternal covenant made between the three persons of the Father, Son, and Holy Spirit. This does not signify three distinct wills in the Trinity but rather distinct personal applications and acts of the one divine will. See Scott R. Swain, "Covenant of Redemption," in *Christian Dogmatics: Reformed Theology for the Church Catholic*, ed. Michael Allen and Scott R. Swain (Grand Rapids: Baker Academic, 2016).

the world's foundation" (John 17:24). Jesus was referring to the covenant of redemption here.[46]

We desperately need redemption in Jesus Christ, as the effects of the fall turned our hearts away from God, with every part of the psychosomatic[47] union of our bodies and souls utterly marred by sin. And sin dehumanizes us. As Kelly Kapic explained, the heart of imaging God is in loving the incarnate Son as the Father does.[48] That is life! And the effects of original sin left us clothed in death. The worst part of that death is a death of love for God. "But God, who is rich in mercy, because of his great love that he had for us, made us alive with Christ even though we were dead in trespasses. You are saved by grace!" (Eph. 2:4–5). Because of the Father's covenant oath with the Son by his Spirit, we see that "in Jesus, God actualizes his call to us to enter communion with him through the Son and by the Spirit."[49] In his incarnation, Jesus did not subtract any part of his divinity, but he humbled himself in that he additionally put on a human nature so that he could fulfill the terms of the covenant of redemption. But our redemption wasn't just some to-do list. It is an outworking of his love in receiving the gift of his bride. Jesus is still fully God and fully man. In this, Jesus can "sympathize with our weaknesses," as he was "tempted in every way as we are, yet without sin" (Heb. 4:15).

As we live in between the already of our redemption and the not yet of our glorification of its consummation, we still feel the weight of sin and shame. We fail to see ourselves as Christ sees us. We need to fight to lay aside our sin and persevere through the race, as the writer to the Hebrews exhorts us. And we do

---

46. See also Ps. 110; Rom. 8:34; Heb. 7:25; 9:24; 1 John 2:1.

47. Mind and body.

48. See Kelly Kapic, "Anthropology," in *Christian Dogmatics: Reformed Theology for the Church Catholic*, ed. Michael Allen and Scott R. Swain (Grand Rapids: Baker Academic, 2016), 166–67.

49. Kapic, 167.

that by fixing "our eyes on Jesus, the pioneer and perfecter of our faith. For the joy that lay before him, he endured the cross, despising the shame, and sat down at the right hand of the throne of God" (12:2). Jesus Christ shows us how to receive a gift, *for the joy that lay before him*. We see him as the first to love, the first to sacrifice, the first to empower.

LOOK TO CHRIST

When we see Christ, our ultimate gift, receiving his bride as a gift of love with the whole story of the covenant of redemption playing out, we have a better grasp of "God's purposes as well as the reality of current human existence—including dignity and struggle, universality and particularity, relationality and personal identity, all understood within the framework of love and communion."[50] Our reality is told in the life of Jesus Christ. Timothy Tennent suggests that our bodies reveal the deep mystery of this covenant of redemption made in eternity. The covenant is prefigured in creation. "God's creation of the body is a physical, representative, and anticipatory preparation of God's grand work in and through the incarnation of Christ. . . . Our created bodies all point to Christ's incarnation, and in turn, his resurrected body points to our physical, bodily (not just spiritual), resurrection at the end of time."[51] Not only that, because of this, his very Spirit is housed in the bodies of his bride.

We learn about our sexuality first, not by looking within ourselves but by looking to Jesus Christ. This is what the Song does, giving us a glorious picture of Jesus, and amazingly, showing us how he views his people/bride. Robert Jenson reminds

---

50. Kapic, 166.
51. Timothy C. Tennent, *For the Body: Recovering a Theology of Gender, Sexuality, and the Human Body* (Grand Rapids: Zondervan Reflective, 2020), 25.

us that "the Song, after its way through theological allegory, provides the chief biblical resource for a believing understanding of human sexuality, the *lived meaning* of 'Male and female he created them.'"[52]

The Song doesn't didactically teach us about sexuality. It avoids the dualistic breakdowns that we love to make of all the ways men and women are different. We don't get the natural law arguments[53] in the Song (that often fail to wrestle with how the fall has distorted them). We don't get assigned roles or hierarchy. We get dignity, eroticism, and freedom told within a grand story of spousal love. The Song isn't meant to flatten the sexes into one-dimensional definitions. It's meant to provoke us in our sexuality to see and long for true love. It provokes us in our own sexuality not to settle for anything less than the love that our bodies were created to speak, warning us not to awaken love until it is ready (Song 2:7; 3:5; 8:4). Let Christ awaken that love so that we can finally love him and others like we should.

Rightly so, the bride begins with "Oh that he would kiss me with the kisses of his mouth!" (Song 1:2). Doesn't that provoke us from the start? She recognizes *the* gift. She needs the gift. We need the kiss of Christ. Isn't it a bit strange that she adds "of his mouth"? How else do we kiss? What is the significance of adding the obvious? Who talks like that? One interpretation, by Honorius of Autun, explains,

52. Robert W. Jenson, *Song of Songs* (Louisville: Westminster John Knox, 2005), 14, emphasis original.

53. See Alastair Roberts, "Can Arguments against Gay Marriage Be Persuasive?," The Calvinist International, March 15, 2013, https://calvinistinter national.com/2013/03/15/can-arguments-against-gay-marriage-be-persuasive/; Patrick Schreiner, "Man and Woman Toward an Ontology," CBMW.org, November 20, 2020, https://cbmw.org/2020/11/20/man-and-woman-toward-an-ontology/; Steven Wedgeworth, "Male-Only Ordination Is Natural: Why the Church Is a Model of Reality, The Calvinist International, January 16, 2019, https://calvinistinter national.com/2019/01/16/male-only-ordination-is-natural-why-the-church-is-a -model-of-reality/.

By **kiss**, then, we understand peace, and by **mouth**, the Word of the Father, that is, the Son. God kissed the bride as it were by someone else's mouth, when formerly "In many and various ways" he spoke "to our fathers by the prophets (Heb. 1:1). He kissed her, so to speak, by his own mouth when "in these last days he spoke to them in the Son" (Heb.1:2), saying "Peace be with you" (John 20:19). For this means: "You will know the peace and the grace, which you lost in the Paradise by agency of the Devil, now restored to you by the agency of my Son."[54]

What a gift is the kiss of the true Groom! We need his kiss to see rightly and to love rightly. But it's plural; she says, "kisses." Kisses are like that, right? They speak a language of their own and therefore multiply. We've been given the kiss of peace, but we still need kisses of Christ's comforting presence now as we go through insecurities, trials, and suffering. Ultimately, we long for that kiss of consummation, when Jesus's prayer to the Father is fully answered and we will be where he is and see him in his glory.

RECOGNIZE YOURSELF IN THE STORY

Are you singing with the bride? Are you longing for the kisses of his mouth? Or are you more like the young women in the Song who seem to mock her with their questions? Like the bride, you may see the reality of who you are without Christ. Not having taken care of your own vineyard, you are dark.

---

54. Honorius of Autun in *The Song of Songs: Interpreted by Early Christian and Medieval Commentators*, trans. and ed. Richard A. Norris Jr., The Church's Bible, paperback ed. (Grand Rapids: Eerdmans, 2019), 23, boldface original.

You've labored for nothing. You have not been loved well by those you put your trust in. But you know about the kisses of his mouth and you are unrelenting in seeking his presence. So you go from singing about him to singing directly to him. His first kiss has called you, giving you access. "Tell me, you whom I love: Where do you pasture your sheep? Where do you let them rest at noon? Why should I be like one who veils herself beside the flocks of your companions?" (Song 1:7). And he answers, "If you do not know, most beautiful of women, follow the tracks of the flock, and pasture your young goats near the shepherds' tents" (Song 1:8).

Do you not know? Augustine asked this question, saying, "*Recognize yourself* for what you are."[55] Most beautiful of women, most fair. Whether a man or a woman, if you are in Christ, you are in a sense the most beautiful of women. If you cannot grasp this, go to God in prayer. If you believe it intellectually but do not feel it in your bones, go to God in prayer. If you do not know because you feel cold to him today, go to God in prayer. He says, "My dove, in the clefts of the rock, in the crevices of the cliff, let me see your face, let me hear your voice; for your voice is sweet, and your face is lovely" (Song 2:14). You need the kisses of his mouth. And you need to be with his flock, his people, the church. We can go directly to God, praying, "This is the body and soul that you gave me to know you. I am created with a longing that can only be satisfied in you. I am made to publicly worship and express witness to your glory. Help me to know this deeply." And then follow the flock. Get with his people. In God's providence, our bodies are covenant-redemptive symbols telling the story of what we were made for: communion with the triune God. This is the most beautiful of women—his church.

---

55. Augustine of Hippo in Norris, *Song*, 50, emphasis original.

RECOGNIZE THE GIFT OF EROTICA

When I threw in the word *eroticism* above, saying that we get dignity, eroticism, and freedom told within a grand story of spousal love, you probably had some sort of reaction. The word does that. The Song of Songs is erotic. That's why some want to say that it is merely allegory and doesn't speak to actual sexual relations and why others say that this book is about sex and marriage and cannot be about God.

There are sexually provocative lines throughout the Song. In it we see the lushness of the garden scenes highlighting the "lushness of sexual exclusivity."[56] The animals in the Song seem to metaphorically participate in the meaningful, erotic intimacy between these lovers. Nature, wildlife, and even we as the readers feel the heat. But there is one line I would have missed had I not read about its reference in a few commentaries. The Bridegroom says, "I compare you, my darling, to a mare among Pharaoh's chariots" (1:9). The thing is, mares were not used with Egyptian chariots. But a tactic has been noted where the opposing general would release a mare in heat as the Pharaoh's stallion-pulled chariots were charging. Robert Jenson sees this simile as giving us a very good picture of what kind of effect the woman had on the Bridegroom: "He took one look and was off"![57] Why would God use such an erotic aspect throughout the Song as analogous to his love for us? Is God using something that we know, like erotic love, to show the power of his love? Jenson says that would be getting it backward: "Human lovers' relations to each other are recognizable in their true eroticism only by noting their analogy to an eroticism that is God's alone."[58]

---

56. Ellen F. Davis, *Proverbs, Ecclesiastes, and the Song of Songs* (Louisville: Westminster John Knox, 2000), 235.

57. Jenson, *Song of Songs*, 26.

58. Jenson, 14.

He compares it to how we know anything about righteousness now—we only know it really by looking to Christ, not to our own feeble attempts at righteousness. Our attempts now are only anticipatory of what is to come.

Peter Leithart explains it like this:

> Sex is allegory, and as allegory it is metaphysics and theology and cosmology. For Christians, sexual difference and union is a type of Christ and the church: How could an erotic poem (and in the Bible!) be anything but allegory? From the Song we relearn that poetic metaphor does not add meaning to what is itself mere chemistry and physics. Nor is erotic poetry a euphemistic cover for Victorian embarrassment. Poetry elucidates the human truth of human sexuality, and it seems uniquely capable of doing so. Only as allegory does the Song have anything to teach us about sex. Only as allegory can the Song play its central role in healing our sexual imaginations.[59]

There's so much to this that we have to learn. So much so, that I feel reductive to get practical here—but I think it important. Our erotic love is to be within covenantal bounds. That is why we uphold sex within marriage between a man and a woman. We are pointing to, anticipating, a covenantal, mutual love between the Creator and his creatures. That's the ultimate distinction. Our own sexual differentiation in marriage tells this story. As Tennent says, "The church cannot marry the church; nor can Christ marry himself."[60] He warns us that adultery, fornication, and gay marriage disfigure this deeper,

---

59. Peter Leithart, "The Poetry of Sex," *First Things*, January 13, 2012, https://www.firstthings.com/web-exclusives/2012/01/the-poetry-of-sex.
60. Tennent, *For the Body*, 52.

theological truth of "the exclusive, unitive sign of our union with Christ as the people of God."[61]

We get erotic love all wrong so much of the time. It's completely self-giving. Christ gave himself for his bride; he loves her to the end (John 13:1). The world's portrayal of erotica is anti-erotica; it's selfish consumption and lust. It's full of shame. The man and the woman in the Song mutually give themselves to one another and are a delight to one another. The whole Song is poetry of delight in one another's presence and longing when separated. It's dripping with anticipatory language like that of the mare among Pharaoh's chariots, "until the day breaks and the shadows flee" (2:17; 4:6).

And that anticipatory language is for singles as well. So is the eros that goes with it. Singles tell the story of the virgin bride, waiting for that day to break. Waiting for the shadows to flee. Waiting for true eros to be consummated. And singles, as Paul said, have an opportunity for more single-minded devotion to the Bridegroom now (1 Cor. 7:32–35).

RECOGNIZE OTHERS AS GIFT

"This is my body, which is given for you" (Luke 22:19). We all should recognize these words of Jesus. We hear them every time we take communion as the body of Christ. This is the ultimate gift. Tennent goes to this eucharistic language, pointing out how this complete, "self-giving, sacrificial love" that Jesus lived out is what "marriage is designed to reflect and image." But it isn't only pictured in marriage. The church as bride should corporately "model this sacrificial and self-giving posture to the world, as we serve the poor and herald the good news of Jesus

---

61. Tennent, 53.

Christ to the lost. The church is the macrocosm; marriage is the microcosm."[62] Tennent makes a profound point here. And he carries it out to the giving of ourselves in service to the needy and the lost. That is what we were when Christ gave himself to us. His example helps us to see our neighbors as gifts—people with dignity, not projects.

But to get this far, we need to be able to see one another in the church as gifts—brothers and sisters. We need communion of persons. Let's circle back to Pope John Paul II's language of self-revelation through the sincere gift of self. God has given us the gift of one another for communion of the saints. How do we welcome our brothers and sisters? Are we giving *ourselves* as gift? And how do we do that? Prudence Allen uses Pope John Paul II's vocational categories in explaining how we are signs to one another: "The married couple together is a living sign of the covenantal body of eternal love; the priest is a living sign of the Bridegroom's love for his bride; and the consecrated person is a living sign of the bride's response to the eternal Bridegroom." In this way, we are all gifts, differentiated by gender and vocational calling, with equal dignity and worth. "Giving of oneself to others and receiving love from others occur in multiple and various ways through chaste friendships and loving relationships in families and neighborhoods, in communities of collaboration, in religious communities, in parishes, in working teams, in organizations, and wherever persons of faith and good will are drawn together for a good and common purpose."[63] I would want to switch out some of the Roman Catholic terms for Protestant ones, but we get the gist of it. Do you see how this posture shows gratitude for God's gifts of brothers and sisters in communion? Do you see the posture of love and how

62. Tennent, 57.
63. Allen, *Concept of Woman*, 3:481–82.

generative and dynamic that would be? Do you see Christ, our Bridegroom, in this?

Do you see how different this is from how I started this chapter? Men and woman are welcomed as gift. There's nothing we have to put on, as our bodies are signs pointing to something much greater than cultural stereotypes and power over others. Our sexuality is enough on its own merit. And yet our sex speaks of the love of the Bridegroom to his beloved. In response, our affections are oriented properly. There is gratitude everywhere. The exclusive, unitive love of Christ will overflow from the church into our households and out onto the streets. It will move us to see Christ through the eyes of others. It will give us appreciation for differentiation, as it glorifies the creativity of our Creator. We were enveloped in darkness and he broke in with his light. Every time we take communion, the words of Jesus should echo out to rattle our own bones and hearts: "This is my body, which is given for you." And we go and do likewise because we belong to him.

QUESTIONS FOR DISCUSSION

1. How does the view taught by the Council on Biblical Manhood and Womanhood that we are to be masculine men and feminine females, acting a certain way to uphold a uniquely feminine or masculine demeanor, contradict the teaching of our sexuality as gift? What does it teach about our metaphysical union of body and soul?

2. Keeping in mind our eternal aim and the typico-symbolic[64] meaning of our sexes, how would upholding Prudence Allen's four demonstratable principles between men and women—equal dignity, significant difference, synergetic relation, and intergenerational fruition—change the way we view, relate to, and invest in one another as disciples in the church?

3. What does this understanding of one another as gift demand of us in our posture and response before God and one another? How does it better uphold the dignity and personhood not only between the sexes but as unique, individual persons?

---

64. The typology of man and woman and symbolism and theology that our bodies represent.

Chapter Six

SOMETIMES THE LAST MAN STANDING IS A WOMAN

"Sometimes, by the grace and power of Jesus, the last man standing is a woman."[1]

I looked at these words that were sent to me as encouragement, wondering if the author of them knew just how prophetic they were. We had both recently been the subject of a YouTube video circulating quickly through social media, titled "Fighting Feminism with Potatoes."[2] We were the two examples of "feminists" in the church who were named in the video. It was released by a Christian publisher, starring one of their popular female authors, in her extravagant kitchen, peeling potatoes for a large gathering in her home. The dining room boasts at least three decked out tables with people already gathering—including her father, the publishing company's founder. In the less than three-minute production, Rachel Jankovic speaks of "encroaching feminism" in the church, and how people like the two of us are leading discussions about whether the Bible really requires that women love their homes. Rather than encouraging

---

1. Beth Moore, personal correspondence.
2. Rachel Jankovic, "Fighting Feminism with Potatoes," *Canon Press*, February 3, 2020, YouTube, https://www.youtube.com/watch?v=5GdLDhXAVwI.

women to meet for intellectual talks about the Bible, writing in its margins while doing word studies, she says that women should love the Bible so much that we are obediently in our homes, writing notes in the margins of our cookbooks. She is doing a horrible job of peeling potatoes while trying to make her case. The video ends with Jankovic saying, "This is the kind of argument that the feminists can never, ever win; because they just can't stand the heat of the kitchen."

Now, I happen to love my home, even though my kitchen sink isn't large enough to have two separate, gorgeous faucets like Jankovic's. I really didn't know how to react to such a video, as the whole thing was a misrepresentation of our writing, name-calling with the Christian f-bomb—*feminist*—and a false dichotomy. We can love our homes *and* study God's Word. (And yet I'm pretty sure that Jesus emphasized sitting at his feet as a disciple over peeling potatoes; see Luke 10:41–42.) There was a part of me—probably not the most Christian part of me—that wanted to respond with a parody video: me, dressed as Peg Bundy from *Married with Children*, peeling my potatoes with a knife (the real way), and a cigarette hanging out of my mouth. But the white angel on my shoulder advised me that I had better things to do with my time.

Anyway, in talking with Beth Moore, the other woman named as an encroaching feminist in the video, we agreed that much worse has been said about us. Thankfully, we have a sense of humor in reacting to a video like this one. Just speaking for myself, I have been slandered, harassed, and plotted against by men and women in the church. Church officers have gone on social media calling me all kinds of names, such as "feminist outrage machine" and "Jezebel," and saying things like if my husband really loved me, he would shut me up. They call ahead of my speaking engagements, warning churches and directors that I am "dangerous" and that they need to guard their families and their churches. Some posted my church's website address on Facebook, telling people they need to call my pastor and elders, demanding they put a stop to me. On and on it goes. So this video, well, it seemed pretty ridiculous. We have to endure much worse—in the church. And it is terribly wrong. But Beth then sent that line of encouragement that inspired the title of this chapter.

I immediately thought of the Song, of course. The last man standing kind of *is* a woman! Collectively. The end of the Song gives us our hope in waiting. Immediately following those heated verses about the fiery flame of Yahweh regarding God's love, the scene switches to mirror the beginning section of the Song.[3] The brothers are fretting about what to do with their sister (8:8–9). The men are having a conversation about what kind of woman their sister is and how to handle her marital fate. But the woman breaks in—interrupts—proclaiming, "I am a wall and my breasts like towers. So in his eyes I have become like one who finds peace" (8:10). We have visited this verse already. It's such a stunning line. We can almost see her standing there. She is a fortress who finds peace in her Bridegroom's eyes. And then she mocks Solomon in her following words: "Solomon owned a vineyard in Baal-hamon. He leased the vineyard to tenants. Each was to bring for his fruit one thousand pieces of silver. I have my own vineyard. The one thousand are for you, Solomon, but two hundred for those who take care of its fruits" (8:11–12).

As Ellen Davis says, Solomon is mocked as "the poor rich man, whose silver and gold are only a foil to show up the superior wealth of love." His many wives foil the "unique value of the one."[4] The woman has declared herself as a city who makes

---

3. For a fascinating argument on the chiastic structuring of the Song, see David A. Dorsey, "Literary Structuring in the Song of Songs," *JSOT* 46 (1990): 81–86.

4. Ellen F. Davis, *Proverbs, Ecclesiastes, and the Song of Songs* (Louisville: Westminster John Knox, 2000), 301.

peace. She is Zion, sister, bride, daughter, and mother of the living. No more do we hear from anyone else in the Song but the bride and her Groom. She is the last woman standing. The bride sees what is real, and it transforms everything. And again, I don't only want to ponder what these ending verses in the Song *mean*; I want to ask, what do they *do*? How does this help the church understand our belonging in Christ, and even that we all are feminine in the sense of our identifying with the bride? The last "man" standing when Christ returns will be his collective bride. How, then, does that belonging inspire us, like the bride, as a fortified holy city, to freely give and receive with those who come to kiss the Son? Hold that thought.

IF ONLY IT WERE A BAD DREAM

I'm sure you've said that before. I don't think we are fully ready to answer the questions above until we go through what the bride went through to get there. There are two "night scenes" in the Song that can be a bit confusing and even disturbing. Some commentators say that they are told like bad dreams. I, for one, am glad that they are in the Song of all songs, the Song given to us in the night. I said earlier that in my own trials, I have found deep comfort in the Song. These night scenes not only tell the story of Israel and the church, but of our own individual spiritual marathons in growth in intimacy with Christ and holiness before him. They can be found in Song 3:1–5 and 5:2–8. Both of them begin with the woman in her bed at night. Both showcase an urgent seeking from the bride and ultimately finding her beloved. She boldly runs into the city in both night scenes, looking for the one her soul loves. The city is portrayed as cold and callous in contrast to the garden and pasture scenes in the Song. Watchmen or guards are present in each scene.

In one they are indifferent and neglectful; in the other they abuse her. Her life is filled with darkness and fret until she finds the beloved.

Absence from the Bridegroom is darkness.

We've been there, right? When we wish a situation was all a bad dream. And the people we seek for help aren't functioning like they should. Whatever the trial, God seems far off. Our affections for him may feel dull. This is the story of the bride too. One difference between the two scenes is that the first one begins with the woman's longing desire for her lover while in her bed alone. It's night. His absence is overwhelming. She wants to be with him. So she is resolute and bold in seeking him. The second scene is different. She is sleeping, and yet she says that her "heart was awake" (Song 5:2). Her beloved comes to her, with the tenderest of words, "my sister, my darling, my dove, my perfect one," asking her to open to him. He's at the door while she is in her bed, but she hesitates. You've probably experienced both of these nights. Sometimes we are aching for the intimacy of God's presence and he feels so distant. Let's be bold like the bride in seeking him. Pray fervently. Go to his Word. Get with his people. Don't stay down. Get up! Other times he is gently prodding us; he is at the door and we hesitate. One can't help but think of this section of the night scene when reading Jesus's words in Revelation 3:20, "See! I stand at the door and knock. If anyone hears my voice and opens the door, I will come in to him and eat with him, and he with me."

I've used the word *echo* over a handful of times while talking about the Song. Distinguishing between direct intertextual references, allusions, and echoes within the canon of Scripture is not an easy art. If the reference is direct, then we will see quoted excerpts from the canon. An allusion to a text could have a partial quote or use some of the same words to make the connection to another text in the canon recognizable.

Scholars disagree on whether such references have to be intentional by the human writer, but they are always intentional by the divine author. Echoes may use a same key word that brings new meaning to the text, or possibly a repeated metaphor or image. Bryan Estelle sums up the discussion: "Some maintain that echoes are less explicit than allusions, just as allusions are less explicit than quotations, whether subtle or direct."[5] These echoes enhance the way we understand a text. Just like allusions, they do not take away from the plain, historical meaning but instead enrich it.

Richard Hays speaks of echoes as "a metaphorical way of talking about a hermeneutical event, an intertextual fusion that generates new meaning."[6] I have tried not to bog down this book with the nuances of distinguishing between all these terms, but I think it is pertinent to note that they play an important part in biblical exegesis. Also, I want to point out how imperative it is for the reader to have what Hays calls a "portable library" of the whole canon to recognize these treasures.[7] In my study of the Song, I'm continually finding new surprises in its many allusions, echoes, and intertextual references. It's like treasure hunting. I just grabbed one from Revelation 3:20, and I want to highlight a few in these night scenes that minister to us in our times of darkness.

Seeking Love

Ellen Davis picks up on quite a few echoes.[8] She notes how the woman describes the man in the first night scene over and over as "the one I love" (Song 3:1, 2, 3, 4; and also in the begin-

---

5. Bryan D. Estelle, *Echoes of Exodus: Tracing a Biblical Motif* (Downers Grove, IL: IVP Academic, 2018), 34.
6. Richard B. Hays, *Echoes of Scripture in the Letters of Paul* (New Haven, CT: Yale University Press, 1989), 23.
7. Hays, 29.
8. See Davis, *Proverbs, Ecclesiastes, and the Song of Songs*, 255–59.

ning of the Song, 1:7). She even describes him that way to the guards, asking if they have seen the one she loves (3:3). Is that really a helpful description? How would they know who she is talking about? But readers should be pulling some references out of the card catalog in their portable library. For example, Deuteronomy 6:5: "Love the LORD your God with all your heart, with all your soul, and with all your strength." And what Jesus confirmed as the greatest commandment: "Love the Lord your God with all your heart, with all your soul, with all your mind, and with all your strength" (Mark 12:30). Similarly, in the second night scene, we see the bride continuously calling her Bridegroom "my love" (Song 5:2, 4, 5, 6, 8). She says she is lovesick (5:8). We are in the night scenes, and yet the bride's words are saturated with Deuteronomic language of the most intense expression. It's the most important thing. Who is she looking for? The one whom her soul loves! The echoes here show us that this is none other than the Lord God!

We see this seeking God theme, or running away from him and after idols instead, throughout the Old Testament. Davis points out some of these verses that are echoed in the woman's anxious search:[9]

> "But from there, you will search for the Lord your God, and you will find him when you seek him with all your heart and all your soul." (Deut. 4:29)

> "You will seek me and find me when you search for me with all your heart." (Jer. 29:13)

> She will pursue her lovers but not catch them;
> she will look for them but not find them.

---

9. Davis, 255–56.

Then she will think,
"I will go back to my former husband,
for then it was better for me than now." (Hos. 2:7)

"I was sought by those who did not ask;
I was found by those who did not seek me.
I said, 'Here I am, here I am,'
to a nation that did not call on my name." (Isa. 65:1)

These verses and more that are evoked by the searching night scenes remind us and the original readers of the call to love God with our whole souls and bodies and warn us not to go after other lovers. And the night scenes show us the fervor with which we should seek him. We have this repeated adjuration not to "stir up or awaken love until the appropriate time" (Song 3:5) in the first night scene. What does this verse do? It makes us pause and ask what we are chasing after. Do we even understand love? When we don't sense God's goodness and love, do we pursue the real thing at all costs, or do we settle for some other gratification? Are we chasing other lovers? Or are we lukewarm, like the church in Laodicea, not realizing we are "wretched, pitiful, poor, blind, and naked" (Rev. 3:17)?

The Wounded Bride

The Song enfleshes the metanarrative of Scripture, reminding us of God's covenant relationship with Israel, including her unfaithfulness. And it bids us now to see Christ as lover of his bride, the church, as we wait in the tension of the already of his betrothal and the not yet of its consummation. The night scenes really highlight this tension. We find an echo in one of the most painful verses in the Song: "The guards who go about the city found me. They beat and wounded me; they took my cloak from me—the guardians of the walls" (5:7).

This is shortly after the wedding scene, in which we are given a peek into the couple's rapturous, consummate satisfaction in lovemaking, and just after the narrator, Yahweh himself, gives the marital blessing: "Eat, friends! Drink, be intoxicated with caresses!" (Song 5:1). While I don't find the Song to be a linear piece, I'm still bothered that it seems to have moved backward here with this night scene. The contrast is so stark. The bride is lovesick and beaten down. Her lover seems nowhere to be found. The Groom who was just praising her, using the very language of sacred space in describing her body with delight, and then who was just at the door calling her sister and dove, hands dripping with dew, seems to have turned his face from her. How can this be in the Song of Songs?

But perhaps this description also gives us hope with its literary allusion—is she echoing from Isaiah in this verse to remind us of the whole story? "For the LORD has called you, like a wife deserted and wounded in spirit, a wife of one's youth when she is rejected," says your God. "I deserted you for a brief moment, but I will take you back with abundant compassion" (54:6–7). This is a comfort to us now, as we are reminded of the abundant compassion of our God. We are loved by God in Christ. We are joined to the Spirit. We need this recalibration when we, too, are gripped by pain, suffering, or sin. We call out to our Groom. And we remember that he has taken all of our woundedness and rejection on himself. As Pope John Paul II beautifully stated it in his *Mulieris Dignitatem*, "Christ is the Bridegroom because 'he has given himself': his body has been 'given,' his blood has been 'poured out' (cf. Lk 22:19–20). In this way 'he loved them to the end' (Jn 13:1). The 'sincere gift' contained in the Sacrifice of the Cross gives definitive prominence to the spousal meaning of God's love. As the Redeemer of the world, Christ is the Bridegroom of the Church."[10]

And we know where to find him. The Song reminds us. When the daughters of Jerusalem ask the bride where her love has gone, she knows the answer: "My love has gone down to his garden, to beds of spice, to feed in the gardens and gather lilies. I am my love's and my love is mine; he feeds among the lilies" (6:2–3). Where is that? Charles Spurgeon rejoiced, saying, "Now, where is Jesus? What are these lilies? Do not these lilies represent the pure in heart, with whom Jesus dwells? The spouse used the imagery which her Lord had put into her mouth. He said, 'As the lily among thorns, so is my love among the daughters,' and she appropriates the symbol to all the saints.'"[11]

The Bridegroom is with his people all along. The Song doesn't only stretch back to Eden; it takes us to the new heavenly garden city. The bride doesn't stay down. She finds her Groom and clings to him. Christ is getting us ready. Things are not as they seem. To behold his bride is to behold "the holy city, the new Jerusalem, coming down out of heaven from God, prepared like a bride adorned for her husband" (Rev. 21:2).

Night Scenes as Polemic

I could go on and on about the night scenes but will just add one more thought and leave you to do your own treasure hunting. Rosalind Clarke notes something painfully obvious about them. Desire costs the woman more than it does the man.[12] She is

---

10. John Paul II, *Mulieris Dignitatem*, apostolic letter, August 15, 1988, §26, http://www.vatican.va/content/john-paul-ii/en/apost_letters/1988/documents/hf_jp-ii_apl_19880815_mulieris-dignitatem.html.

11. Charles Haddon Spurgeon, "A Song among the Lilies (SS 2:16)," in *Charles Spurgeon on the Song of Solomon: 64 Sermons to Ignite a Passion for Jesus!* Christian Classics Treasury (2013), Kindle ed., loc. 5110.

12. See Rosalind S. Clarke, "Canonical Interpretations of the Song of Songs" (PhD diss., University of Aberdeen, 2013), 217, https://eu03.alma.exlibrisgroup.com/view/delivery/44ABE_INST/12152788870005941.217.

vulnerable in the city while seeking the one she loves. We see it in that painful verse about abuse from the guards, which I shared above. Both night scenes have the same line: "The guards who go about the city found me" (3:3; 5:7). They neglect her appeal for help in the first night scene. The bride asks them if they've seen the one whom her soul loves, and we don't hear a response. She passes them and finds her lover on her own. But in the second scene, they beat her, wound her, strip her of her cloak—"the guardians of the walls" (5:7). We get this sense of a reoccurring dream, the scene recapitulated with compounded abuse. She is exposed and vulnerable, confronted by violence from male authority. It really bothers us because her beloved isn't harmed like this in the Song. He doesn't step in here. Clarke suggests this adds to the adjuration to the daughters of Jerusalem[13]—desire includes suffering for the sake of the Beloved. Count the cost.

Again, we don't just find meaning in this text, it *does* something. Clarke suggests that the bride's voice is speaking for all those who have been oppressed and abused. The woman shares her experience, bringing darkness to light. She isn't silent. The young women then ask her what makes her lover better than others (Song 5:9). Why go through this? How is this man different from the guards or all the other patriarchal abusers women have suffered under? Why should they help her look for this man? The bride answers with a *wasf* that begins, "My beloved is white and ruddy, Chief among ten thousand" (5:10 NKJV). John Owen highlighted, "He is *white* in the glory of his *Deity*, and *ruddy* in the preciousness of his *humanity*. . . . He who was white, became ruddy for our sakes, pouring out his blood as an oblation for sin. This also renders him graceful: by his whiteness he fulfilled the law; by his redness he satisfied justice."[14] (And here's

---

13. Clarke, 218.
14. John Owen, *Communion with God* (1657; repr., Oxford: Benediction Classics, 2017), 49–50.

another treasure—that whiteness is echoed in the description of Christ in Rev. 1:14.) The beginning of the bride's description points to the One who has suffered for us and is able to save.

So what does that do? Clarke elaborates:

> This woman speaks, in some sense, for all women who have been oppressed and abused. In the context of the Writings,[15] this includes the women who were evicted from their homes and families as the result of Ezra's edict, and the women who were written out of Israel's history in Chronicles. Denied any voice or identity elsewhere in the Writings, women who identify with these experiences find a representative in this woman. . . . Her suffering can stand for theirs and her voice for theirs, not only in her suffering, but in her desire.[16]

The bride's description exposes the darkness and moves us to the true orientation of desire—to the One who felt our pain, took on our shame, poured out his blood, and clothed us in his righteousness. Desire cost him the most, for it was for the joy set before him that he endured the cross (Heb. 12:2). The bride's description of her Beloved has similarities to his *wasf* describing her when they wed (Song 4:1–7). She sees herself in him. She has counted the cost, and she is telling the young women—and us— that he is worth it! This text evangelizes, inviting us to participate in this kind of dangerous desire that brings us to our great reward.[17]

The night scenes can function as a polemic against what has played out in history since the fall. Sin has brought the worst

---

15. The Hebrew Bible (Tanakh) classified books by the Torah (Law, Pentateuch), Nevi'im (Prophets), and Ketuvim (Writings). The Writings made up the poetry and wisdom literature: Psalms, Proverbs, and Job; the Five Scrolls, or Megillot: Song of Songs, Ruth, Lamentations, Ecclesiastes, and Esther (read in the synagogue in this order on holidays); and the books of Daniel, Ezra and Nehemiah, and Chronicles.

16. Clarke, "Canonical Interpretations," 218.

17. See Clarke, 219.

kind of corruption, showcased so poignantly in the abuse of women. If we do not love the Lord with our souls and our bodies, then we surely are not going to love his bride. This polemic climaxes in the second night scene, but it plays out in the whole Song. As Clarke puts it, "Alone in the streets, exploited in her brother's vineyards, or mocked by the daughters of Jerusalem, she has been vulnerable throughout, even to those who ought to have protected her."[18] The bride is vulnerable. But she perseveres because the Bridegroom is preserving her. In going through the night scene experiences and overcoming to the end, she is transformed. She is radiant. She is a wall. She sees real love, which is "as strong as death" (8:6).

The bride echoes King David, "I wait for the LORD; I wait and put my hope in his word. I wait for the LORD more than the watchmen for the morning—more than the watchmen for the morning" (Ps. 130:5–6). In the Song we get a glimpse of the consummation of this hope that is held by Christ's people "until the day breaks and the shadows flee" (2:17; 4:6).

STANDING FOR HOPE

We get another glimpse of the consummation of this hope in Revelation. Nicholas Batzig makes the bold claim, "It is my contention that John used the entire background of the love/worship imagery of the Song as an echo in the Apocalypse."[19] Reverberating echoes! One of his examples is found in Revelation 14:4. The scene is set with the Lamb among his redeemed people on Mount Zion. They are singing a new song

---

18. Clarke, 222.
19. Nicholas Batzig, "John's Use of the Song of Songs in the Book of Revelation," *Feeding on Christ* (blog), July 1, 2013, https://feedingonchrist.org/johns-use-of-the -song-of-songs-in-the-book-of-revelation/.

before the throne. (Is this really a brand-new song or the Song of Songs made new, made complete and true? I don't know, but I digress.) Who are the redeemed? "These are the ones who have not defiled themselves with women, since they remained virgins. These are the ones who follow the Lamb wherever he goes. They were redeemed from humanity as the firstfruits for God and the Lamb" (Rev. 14:4). This echo actually begins to ring in the Wedding Psalm, 45:14: "In colorful garments she is led to the king; after her, the virgins, her companions, are brought to you." Ah, yes, "no wonder young women adore you" (Song 1:3). Remember the woman wanting to know where to find the Bridegroom, calling out to him (1:7)? He graciously replies, "If you do not know, most beautiful of women, follow the tracks of the flock, and pasture your young goats near the shepherds' tents" (1:8). This is echoed in Revelation 14:4. Batzig says the usage of the word *virgin* in Revelation is an "allusive allusion." "If they were sexually and morally pure, why would they need to follow the Lamb (signifying the saving work of the One who was slain for sinners)? Because they are following Christ, who died for their sins, they are made spiritually faithful (and in that sense can be called 'virgins'), in contrast to being spiritual adulterers (see Matt. 12:39 and 16:4)."[20] Who are the ones standing and singing as the redeemed bride in the Apocalypse? Both the Song and Revelation identify them as the spiritually faithful who follow the Lamb who is also the Shepherd.

Batzig notes other echoes, such as reading Song 5:10–16 in light of Revelation 1:12–16, and the knocking on the door in Revelation 3:20 as an echo of Song of Songs 5:2. But more than just specific verses, John echoes the themes and metaphors in the Song. "Both books are interested in the believer's experiential communion with Him during the waiting period."[21]

20. Batzig, "John's Use of the Song."
21. Batzig, "John's Use of the Song."

We can identify with this, as we are in that waiting period. We need this encouragement and hope, this eschatological vision. Additionally, Batzig notes themes of

> love/longing, as it is seen against the background of absence/presence. Both begin with a declaration of the Bridegroom's love. Both conclude with an expressed longing for the Bridegroom to appear. Both books center on the dwelling of the Bridegroom with his Bride. Geographical locations are used symbolically in both books. The spatial nomenclatures that are applied to the characters of the Song serve to reveal the archetypal fulfillment of the prototypes. [That is, the names that are given to the man and the woman of the Song reveal a typology that we see fulfilled in Revelation.] For instance, both books employ Garden-Temple-City language to describe the lovers. The identification of the Church as Garden-City in the Apocalypse is set forth in its eschatological fulfillment. Nothing less should be expected from the apex of covenantal revelation.[22]

And with these additional themes and metaphors we see something else. The hope of the bride is tied to the hope of the land. The metaphors are so tied together that they reveal this typology of woman—sacred space, the second order, restored land, restored Israel, church, bride, mother of the living. The Song echoes Isaiah and Hosea on this as well. I don't have the space to cover it all, as it could be a book of its own. But briefly, let's begin with an outline of some fascinating echoes in just two chapters of Isaiah.[23] First, the land/bride echoes and allusions from Isaiah 35 are astounding:

---

22. Batzig, "John's Use of the Song." Parenthetical explanation added.
23. Also see Clarke, "Canonical Interpretations," 161–64.

Isaiah 35:1	**Song of Songs 2:1**
The desert will rejoice and blossom like a *wildflower*.	I am a *wildflower* of Sharon, a lily of the valleys.

Isaiah 35:2	**Song of Songs 2:1; 2:12; 4:8**
It will *blossom* abundantly and will also rejoice with joy and *singing*. The glory of *Lebanon* will be given to it, the splendor of Carmel and *Sharon*. They will see the glory of the LORD, the splendor of our God.	I am a wildflower of *Sharon*. The *blossoms* appear in the countryside. The time of *singing* has come. Come with me from *Lebanon* my bride, come with me from *Lebanon*!

Isaiah 35:6	**Song of Songs 4:15**
Then the lame will leap like a deer, and the tongue of the mute will sing for joy, for *water will gush* in the wilderness, and streams in the desert.	You are a garden spring, a well of *flowing water streaming* from Lebanon.

Isaiah 35:9	**Song of Songs 4:8**
There will be no *lion* there . . . but the redeemed will walk on [the Holy Way].	Descend from . . . the dens of the *lions*.

Isaiah 35:10	**THE WHOLE SONG!** **Song of Songs 3:11**
And the redeemed of the LORD will return and come to *Zion* with singing, *crowned* with unending joy. *Joy and gladness* will overtake them, and sorrow and sighing will flee.	Go out, young women of *Zion*, and gaze at King Solomon, wearing the *crown* his mother placed on him on the day of his wedding— the day of his *heart's rejoicing*.

As Rosalind Clarke elucidates, restored land *is* restored Israel. The bride in the Song is connected to this land imagery.[24] Israel/bride/church—their hope is the same. Additionally, I love the meditation from Owen on that last verse, Song 3:11: "It is the day of his coronation, and his spouse is the crown

---

24. Clarke, 162–63.

wherewith he is crowned. For as Christ is a diadem of beauty and a crown of glory unto Zion, Isa. xxviii.5; so Zion is also a diadem and a crown unto him, Isa. lxii.3."[25] The crown echoes reverberate our value to Christ and the rejoicing that is mutually ours in the consummation of Zion. Let's look at another chapter with strong echoes, Isaiah 62:

Isaiah 62:1
I will not keep silent because of Zion, and I will not keep still because of Jerusalem, until her righteousness *shines like a bright light* and her salvation *like a flaming torch.*

Song of Songs 6:10; 8:6
Who is this who *shines like the dawn,* as beautiful as the *moon, bright as the sun.*
     Love's flames are *fiery flames* —an *almighty flame!*

Isaiah 62:2
Nations will see your righteousness and all kings, your glory. You will be given a *new name* that the LORD's mouth will announce.

Song of Songs 6:13
Come back, come back, *Shulammite!* Come back, come back *that we may look at you! How you gaze* at the *Shulammite, as you look* at the dance of the two camps!

Isaiah 62:3
You will be *a glorious crown* in the LORD's hand.

Song of Songs 3:11
Go out, young women of Zion, and gaze at King Solomon, *wearing the crown his mother placed on him* on the day of his wedding —the day of his heart's rejoicing.

Isaiah 62:4
You will no longer be called Deserted, and your land will not be called Desolate; instead, you will be called *My Delight is in Her,* and your land Married; for *the LORD delights in you,* and your land will be married.

Song of Songs 7:6
How beautiful you are and how pleasant, *my love, with such delights!*

---

25. Owen, *Communion with God*, 55.

Isaiah 62:5
For as a young man marries
a young woman, so your sons
will marry you; and *as a groom
rejoices over his bride, so your God
will rejoice over you.*

Song of Songs 3:11; 4:7, 9
*On the day of his wedding—the day
of his heart's rejoicing.*
*You are absolutely beautiful,
my darling; there is no imperfection
in you.*
*You have captured my heart,
my sister, my bride.*

Isaiah 62:8
*Foreigners will not drink the new
wine for which you have labored.*

Song of Songs 8:2
I would lead you, I would take
you, to the house of my mother
who taught me. *I would give you
spiced wine to drink from the juice of
my pomegranate.*

Isaiah 62:10
Prepare a way for the people! . . .
Raise a *banner* for the peoples.

Song of Songs 6:4, 10
You are as beautiful as Tirzah, my
darling, lovely as Jerusalem, *awe-
inspiring as an army with banners.*
Who is this . . . *awe-inspiring as
an army with banners?*

Isaiah 62:11
Look, the LORD has proclaimed
to the ends of the earth, "Say
to Daughter Zion: Look, your
salvation is coming, *his wages
are with him, and his reward
accompanies him.*"

Song of Songs 8:12
I have my own vineyard. The one
thousand are for you, Solomon,
but two hundred for those who
take care of its fruits.

Isaiah 62:12
And they will be called the Holy
People, the LORD's Redeemed;
and you will be called Cared For,
A City Not Deserted.

**Song of Songs 6:4 (in contrast
to the night scenes)**
*You are as beautiful as Tirzah,
my darling, lovely as Jerusalem.*

The bride stands in hope of these promises of God. I could
have grabbed more, pondering on other themes of wine, watchmen, and gates, but I tried to pull out the louder echoes that can
speak fairly easily for themselves when coupled. Perhaps you are

picking up some more echoes in Revelation from these verses. This is where we see our hope fulfilled. The Song reverberates more echoes from Isaiah, such as the song of the vineyard in chapter 5. Because of space concerns, I now want to jump to Hosea. There are multiple echoes there as well, particularly the overall story of the bride and her Groom. But look at what Clarke has drawn out just from Hosea 14, with the connected theme of restoration in the bourgeoning land:

אהב love	Hosea 14:4	Song 1:3, 4, 7; 3:1, 2, 3, 4
טל dew	Hosea 14:5	Song 5:2
פרה to blossom	Hosea 14:5, 7	Song 6:11; 7:13
שׁוֹשָׁן lily	Hosea 14:5	Song 2:1, 2, 16; 4:5; 5:13; 6:2, 3; 7:3
נכה to take (root)	Hosea 14:5	Song 5:7
לבנון Lebanon	Hosea 14:5, 6, 7	Song 3:9; 4:8, 11, 15; 5:15; 7:5
ריח scent	Hosea 14:6	Song 1:3, 12; 2:13; 4:10, 11; 7:9, 14
יָשַׁב to dwell	Hosea 14:7	Song 2:3; 5:12; 8:13
צל shadow	Hosea 14:7	Song 2:3, 14; 4:6
גפן vine	Hosea 14:7	Song 2:13; 6:11; 7:9, 13
זכר remembrance	Hosea 14:7	Song 1:4
יין wine	Hosea 14:7	Song 1:2, 4; 2:4; 4:10; 5:1; 7:10; 8:2[26]

With all this likeness and echoing of land and bride language, there is still an interesting difference. While much of Hosea plays on this bride metaphor for Israel, the language in the last chapter is masculine. Israel is portrayed as a man here. The metaphor somewhat changes to the orphan, "the fatherless" receiving compassion (14:3), even as the bridal echoes are

---

26. Clarke, "Canonical Interpretations," 165.

picked up in the Song. What's going on here? Francis Landy sheds light on the complexities:

> One would expect Israel to be the female partner; grammatically, however, it remains obstinately masculine, as do most of the images. The masculinity is presumably inclusive, comprising Israel as male and female subject. Nevertheless, the elimination of the feminine persona has the effect of desexing the Song; Israel is as much orphan/child as lover. In 13.13–14.1, the grammatical masculinity of Ephraim maintains a semblance of social normality, reducing the figure of travailing mother to metaphor and enabling it to be mother and son at the same time. Here the sexual tensions of the poem are neutralized in part through projection onto the fantasy realm of Lebanon, and in part through making them as ethereal, and as carefully disguised, as possible.[27]

I can only partially wrap my head around this. But it's what I've been saying all along: women point to our telos as Christ's bride, and men to our telos as sons in the Son. The last man standing—the adopted son of God—is also the bride of Christ. Both men and women claim this eschatological status, all without losing our sexual distinctions in our own sexuate installations as men and as women. We stand with a shared and sure hope!

STANDING STRONG

I don't know how many women today would be turned on before lovemaking if her groom told her that her neck was like a tower. But the Groom in the Song goes for it, telling her, "Your

---

27. Francis Landy, *Hosea*, 2nd ed., Readings: A New Biblical Commentary, ed. John Jarick (Sheffield: Sheffield Phoenix Press, 2011), 202.

neck is like the tower of David, constructed in layers. A thousand shields are hung on it—all of them shields of warriors" (4:4). Her neck is likened to a military structure.[28] We see the advantage of a tower throughout the Old Testament canon. As Carol Meyers explains, "Whether as an isolated structure in the field (Isa 5:2; Mic 4:9; Gen 35:21) or as the stronghold of a city (Judg 9:46–49; Neh 3:1; 12:39), a tower represents strength and protection."[29] Meyers notes how we don't ever read about an actual tower of David, *the* military commander extraordinaire, so this is more of an abstraction.[30] It would be the tower of towers. In this verse, this sweet nothing whispered to the bride before lovemaking on her wedding night associates her neck with top-notch military language: tower, David, a *thousand* shields, warriors. This is how the Groom sees her.

The word *tower* pops back up again in another *wasf* about the bride. Here he says that her neck is a tower of ivory, and her nose is "like the tower of Lebanon looking toward Damascus" (7:4). This Damascus reference is again alluding to military advantage, whether referring to an actual tower or to the mountains of Damascus being towering. Damascus was situated on a high plateau and was a "major military threat to Israel between the reign of Solomon and the Assyrian conquest in 732 B.C.E."[31] Meyers continues regarding the military language used in Song 7:4: "The 'pools' in Hebron to which the woman's eyes are likened are most likely artificial pools—reservoirs—constructed for military, not agricultural, purposes (Paul and Dever, 1973, pp. 127–43). And the 'gate' of Bat Rabbim is part

---

28. This reminds us of the military language saturated around the word helper/ *ezer* that is first used to describe women as man's *ezer* (Gen. 2:18), and also used to describe God as Israel's *ezer* (Ex. 18:4; Deut. 33:7, 26, 29; Pss. 20:2; 33:20; 70:5; 89:17; 115:9–11; 121:1–2; 124:8; 146:5; Hos. 13:9).

29. Carol Meyers, "Gender Imagery in the Song of Songs," *HAR* 10 (1986): 213, https://core.ac.uk/download/pdf/159572290.pdf.

30. Meyers, 213.

31. Meyers, 214.

of the military defenses of a city and also a public place, a place frequented by males (cf. Prov 31:23) and not by females."[32] What is all this about? How does this challenge our own view of gender imagery?

We all know where I'm going. Well, I would hope so after all the harping I've done on Song 8:10. There she is, standing strong, using her own voice to describe herself as a wall. Now her breasts are towers. Something that is associated with male desire and motherly nurture is described as a militant force. And another plot twist: "The one to whom all the military allusions have been made secures the opposite of what they represent."[33] In his eyes she finds peace. But that is just it. All this military language from the male world ascribed to the woman and her own appropriation of it goes back to what Anna Anderson says about our symbolic nature—the homecoming after the war.[34] Woman is a type of the second order. Grasping this typology, really understanding it, changes how we see. Is not that the advantage of the tower? Perspective! Sight! What strength there is against enemies and temptation in the advantage of sight!

Peter implores husbands to treat their wives with honor, as they are the weaker vessel (1 Peter 3:7). Is this a contradiction? No, Peter is likely referring to the physical differences women have in strength, but mostly in conjunction to their resulting status in the world. Men throughout history have held their power over women, and Peter says, *No, you are heirs together and your own prayers will be hindered if you treat your wife the way the world does. See her as Christ sees his bride. Her whole body and presence points you to true strength—in receiving the love of the Lord, you have the strongest advantage. Her very breasts point to your absolute dependence on her for life, just like the collective bride is absolutely*

32. Meyers, 214.
33. Meyers, 215.
34. See p. 125.

dependent on Christ, who nurtures her by his Word and sacrament in his church. She sees. She feeds. She is a city on a hill (Matt. 5:14).

Her neck is a tower in this world. It holds the head and sets the eyes in the direction in which they will see. Her nose is a tower of Lebanon, for the church. It has the best vantage position—others have to align themselves with her to secure peace. And her breasts are towers. She has found peace in the eyes of her Beloved and is sharing her strength with her brothers and sisters, feeding them with the Word. This is the church. Zion. The last woman standing.

SING WITH ME

After I spoke with a group of church leaders once on the topic of discipling men and women in the church, one pastor took me aside. He didn't want to make his comment during the Q&A session we had just finished. He told me that my message had merit, but he was concerned about the feminization of the church and he wanted my thoughts on that. Wasn't I worried that investing in more women would lead to this? Anecdotally, he said that he'd noticed that women were eager to learn; and the more churches invest in them, the more they will rise in leadership over the men. Or in influencing the men. Which feminizes the church.

Have you heard something like this before? I'm guessing so, because I hear it often. Pastors go on the internet, writing articles like "On Getting and Keeping Masculine Men in the Church," with advice on how to attract "manly men" in your congregation "that will likely trigger the feminists among [his] readers."[35] The problem this pastor is addressing is that too

---

35. C. R. Wiley, "On Getting and Keeping Masculine Men in the Church," *Paterfamilias[Daily]* (blog), Patheos, January 29, 2018, https://www.patheos.com /blogs/gloryseed/2018/01/on-getting-keeping-masculine-men-in-church/.

many churches—not his—have a ratio of significantly more women than men in the church. Horror of horrors.

I remember thinking, *Not you too!*, when an author whom I respected wrote a well praised and circulated article titled "Hysteria and the Need for Male Leadership."[36] The title alone is disturbing. It reduces women to a term loaded with historical baggage. Based on the Greek word for uterus, hysteria refers to extreme irrationality and excessive emotion, lacking logic. The title portrays that since uteruses cause women to have "ungovernable emotional excess,"[37] women cannot lead. And that is the case he makes: "Men must build their brotherhoods again, from the ground up, and be once again, if unacknowledged, the legislators of our common life."[38] Women are a threat and must be managed. Now, this was not an article about church, but his writing is faith-informed, and he is a well-respected author in my religious circles, even as he is a Roman Catholic. As goes the church, so goes the world, they say.

Feminization has been a "threat" to the church for a while now. Books like *The Church Impotent: The Feminization of Christianity*,[39] *Why Men Hate Going to Church*,[40] and *The Masculine Mandate: God's Calling to Men*[41] identify the problem and offer solutions. The internet buzzed after a popular Desiring God con-

---

36. Anthony Esolen, "Hysteria and the Need for Male Leadership," *The New English Review*, November, 2018, https://www.newenglishreview.org/custpage. cfm?frm=189446&sec_id=189446&fbclid=IwAR2hsnHjfyIh9O0f0uEYE8kBsj1ASB 94aiBBxrS1A2YOnWena4ITDSHbbRw. See Aimee Byrd, "A Response to Anthony Esolen Regarding Women and Hysteria," *Aimee Byrd* (blog), November 2, 2018, https://aimee byrd.com/2020/06/13/a-response-to-anthony-esolen-regarding-women-and-hysteria/.

37. "Hysteria," Wikipedia, accessed December 10, 2020, https://en.wikipedia .org/wiki/Hysteria.

38. Esolen, "Hysteria and the need for Male Leadership."

39. Leon J. Podles, *The Church Impotent: The Feminization of Christianity* (Dallas, TX: Spence, 1999).

40. David Murrow, *Why Men Hate Going to Church*, rev. and updated ed. (Nashville: Thomas Nelson, 2011).

41. Richard Phillips, *The Masculine Mandate: God's Calling to Men* (Sanford, FL: Reformation Trust, 2016).

ference honoring J. C. Ryle, titled "God, Manhood, and Ministry," where John Piper claimed, "God has given Christianity a masculine feel. . . . From which I infer that the fullest flourishing of women and men takes place in churches and families where Christianity has this God-ordained, masculine feel. For the sake of the glory of women, and for the sake of the security and joy of children, God has made Christianity to have a masculine feel. He has ordained for the church a masculine ministry."[42]

Earlier I referred to the popular resource from CBMW published to combat "evangelical feminism" and prefaced by urging the need for "masculine males" and "feminine females." Since its publication, there have been many articles and talks regarding a so-called "crisis going on in the local church. Number one, men aren't coming. And number two, when they are coming, they're marginalized, they're being passive, they're being pushed to the side."[43] Robert Stinson spoke on this at a lecture sponsored by the Southern Baptist Theological Seminary, lamenting, "The current feminization of Christianity reflects a larger trend in pop culture where women are pushed to be more masculine and men are pushed to be more feminine." What must we do to fix this crisis? *"Pastors must exercise assertive male leadership to guide their churches away from a feminized Christianity."* So, the problems in the church are feminine. Women, with their softness and emotiveness are taking over, freaking the manly men out. Men cannot continue to flourish under the feminine ways of doing things. "They get stuff done."[44]

What's to sing about here? I don't see anywhere in Scripture

---

42. John Piper, "The Frank and Manly Mr. Ryle: The Value of a Masculine Ministry," God, Manhood and Ministry: Building Men for the Body of Christ, Desiring God 2012 Conference for Pastors, January 31, 2012, https://www.desiringgod.org/messages/the-frank-and-manly-mr-ryle-the-value-of-a-masculine-ministry.

43. CBMW Editors, "Feminine Christianity Turns Men Away from Church, CBMW Executive Director Says," CBMW, April 18, 2006, https://cbmw.org/2006/04/18/feminine-christianity-turns-men-away-from-church-cbmw-executive-director-says/.

44. CBMW, "Feminine Christianity Turns Men Away," emphasis original.

where there are warnings about the growing number of women joining the church over men. I don't see Paul worried that because Timothy was brought up in the faith by his grandma and mother, he might be too soft. No, he was thankful for Lois and Eunice passing down the faith (2 Tim. 1:5). We read nothing about Timothy being feminized because of it.

Scot McKnight challenges this notion of masculine feel that Piper espouses as unbiblical:

> There is a Greek word for "masculine" (*andreia*); it never occurs in the New Testament (a word close to it occurs in 1 Cor 16:13, but seems to be addressing the whole church—and means courage). Nor does it appear once in any words quoted here of J. C. Ryle. This is a colossal example of driving the whole through a word ("masculine") that is not a term used in the New Testament, which Testament never says "For Men Only." Pastors are addressed in a number of passages in the NT, and not once are they told to be masculine.[45]

We seem to be forgetting that the first churches met in households. Talk about feminizing! And in Scripture we see mainly women hosting these house churches: Prisca (Rom. 16:3–5; 2 Tim. 4:19), Chloe (1 Cor. 1:11), Nympha (Col. 4:15), Apphia (Philem. 1:2), Lydia (Acts 16:40), Junia (Rom. 16:7), and Phoebe (Rom. 16:1–2). Despite attempts to polarize the influence of women as purely domestic and never public, Carolyn Osiek and Margaret MacDonald note how these "categories are overdrawn and often too rigidly applied."[46] Furthermore, Susan Hylen demonstrates that scholars have often read anachronisti-

---

45. Scot McKnight, "John Piper, What He Said," *Jesus Creed* (blog), Patheos, February 3, 2012, https://www.patheos.com/blogs/jesuscreed/2012/02/03/john-piper-what-he-said/.

46. Carolyn Osiek and Margaret Y. MacDonald with Janet H. Tulloch, *A Woman's Place: House Churches in Earliest Christianity* (Minneapolis: Fortress, 2006), 3.

cally when imposing a division in gender roles in Greco-Roman societies based on *modern* notions of private and public. While today we closely associate "public sphere" with "public action" (whereas everything "private" belongs in the home), in the first century, such association did not exist. "Private" often signified proprietary interest and did not necessarily delineate location. Many more activities were classified as "private" than we may think, including commerce, education, and business, and many of these were conducted in public spaces. Sacred spaces were distinguished from public spaces, and household spaces often held public functions, depending on the occupant's social status. Women were not confined to merely "domestic" activities, but freely moved around and participated in public spaces in judicial, commercial, sacred, and political spheres.[47]

We see what is written about women (or not) by those who want to influence society. But we also need to take into consideration historical evidence from everyday living, such as personal letters, receipts, legal documents, invitations, or even architectural or burial inscriptions. These historical finds reveal that women's public agency and influence are more complex than what we find in "published" writings. We have evidence of women interacting and contributing in the home, society, and even in the synagogue, as elements such as location and needs of the community factor into a woman's opportunities for education, commerce, and religious service.[48] Even so, we cannot deny "the domestic flavor that would have permeated Christian meetings."[49] The everyday cares of household life are part of the beautiful, busy matrix of gathered worship. Osiek and MacDonald go so far as to say that since women managed

---

47. See Susan Hylen, "Public and Private Space and Action in the Early Roman Period," *NTS* 66 (2020): 534–53.

48. See Lynn H. Cohick, *Women in the World of the Earliest Christians* (Grand Rapids: Baker Academic, 2009), 322–23.

49. Osiek and MacDonald, *Woman's Place*, 246.

all that went on in the household, "to step into a Christian house church was to step into women's world."[50]

What if a larger percentage of women in the church was a good thing? What if their contributions and influence were fruitful and not feared? What if the very presence of female bodies spoke something glorious to God's people? Rodney Stark argues that "the rise of Christianity *depended* upon women."[51] Like it or not, "the early church drew substantially more female than male converts, and this in a world where women were in short supply."[52] Likewise, Peter Lampe elucidates, "That Christianity found a hearing predominantly among women in Rome and elsewhere is sufficiently known and testified."[53] Stark argues that women made up around two-thirds of the early church, although we really do not have concrete evidence for these demographics. This was at a time, according to Stark, when more than two-thirds of the population were men— around 70 percent! He attributes the shortage of women to their devaluation, revealed by high levels of female infanticide. Even large families usually kept only one daughter. On top of that, the mortality rate during childbirth was high. And yet the church valued women. And women responded. Because of the Christian value for life, abortion and infanticide were condemned in the church. Exclusive, covenantal love in marriage was promoted. Husbands often converted to Christianity via their wives, what Stark calls "secondary conversions." Even when the husbands

---

50. Osiek and MacDonald, *Woman's Place*, 163.

51. Rodney Stark, *The Triumph of Christianity: How the Jesus Movement Became the World's Largest Religion* (New York: HarperCollins, 2011), e-book, 159, emphasis added. In contrast, Larry Hurtado says a contributing factor to the demise of the cult of Mithras was the exclusion of women. Larry W. Hurtado, *Destroyer of the Gods: Early Christian Distinctiveness in the Roman World* (Waco, TX: Baylor University Press, 2016), 84.

52. Stark, 159.

53. Peter Lampe, *From Paul to Valentinus: Christians at Rome in the First Two Centuries* (Philadelphia: Fortress, 2003), 146.

didn't convert, their children were still raised in the church and considered holy (1 Cor. 7:14).[54] Stark concludes, "Having an excess of women gave the church a remarkable advantage because it resulted in disproportionate Christian fertility and in a considerable number of secondary conversions."[55] No one was complaining about the feminization of the church.

But we don't need merely to conclude that women outnumbered the men because they were valued more there. Osiek and MacDonald argue that there was a simultaneous movement in Roman society, not in the modern sense of liberation for women, but one that did begin opening doors for some social freedoms for women.[56] There were other options. Women were valued in Christianity, but even more so, they began to see what is most valuable. As Judith Lieu observes, women may have converted for intellectual reasons as well.[57] To take it a step further, intellectual stimulation and contribution are sparked by the grace of God. Providentially, Christ was given to and received by many women, and they responded with their bodies, minds, and souls. What matters most is that Christ is preached and nurtured in his people. Imagine that.

When someone starts talking about the feminization of the church, it is an instant sign to me that they don't see. They don't have the perspective of the tower. Consistently, we see that even today there are more women in the church than men. Around the world, studies show that more women attend church, pray, and deem their faith important to their lives.[58] This brings me back to my earlier question about what the ending verses in the

---

54. Stark, *Triumph*, 141–59.
55. Stark, *Triumph*, 159.
56. Osiek and MacDonald, *Woman's Place*, 2.
57. Judith Lieu, "The Attraction of Women in/to Early Judaism and Christianity: Gender and the Politics of Conversion," *JSNT* 72 (1998): 5–22.
58. "The Gender Gap in Religion around the World," Pew Research Center, March 22, 2016, https://www.pewforum.org/2016/03/22/the-gender-gap-in-religion-around-the-world/.

Song do. They point us to Christ and to the last woman standing. Immediately, I am reminded of other women standing in Scripture, whose lives also point to the Bridegroom and call us to him:

- Tamar, who exposed Judah's hypocrisy while fighting to secure his progeny in the ancestry of Christ (Gen. 38)
- Shiphrah and Puah, who defied Pharaoh and kept the male Hebrew line alive (Ex. 1:15–21)
- Abigail, who brought needed hospitality to David and his men, interceding at the risk of her own life, recognizing his kingship and imploring him to leave vengeance to God (1 Sam. 25)
- Rahab, who hid the spies, recognizing that God was giving Israel the land, and securing herself into God's covenant family (Josh. 2)
- Ruth, who grasped God's *hesed* love in fulfilling the vow she made to Naomi, securing a son in the line of Christ (Ruth)
- Esther, the foreign wife of the king, who by faith approached the king in the inner court without invitation to be a whistleblower, saving God's people from annihilation (Esther)
- Anna the prophetess, who waited into old age for the Holy One, whom she saw with her own eyes, telling anyone who would listen that redemption had come (Luke 2:36–38)
- The Canaanite woman who followed Jesus's flock to find him after he withdrew from crowds, relentlessly asking for healing for her daughter, showing her great faith in theological conversation with Jesus, and foreshadowing the Great Commission he was later to proclaim (Matt. 15:21-28)

- The Samaritan woman, who like the Deuteronomy 24 woman, was passed from husband to husband, such that her own body, which was to represent sacred space, had been defiled, and who had no real husband now, called her whole town to the betrothing well with the true Bridegroom (John 4:7–42)
- Martha, who ran ahead to meet Jesus after the death of her brother, and when confronted by him on true life and death, professed that he was "the Messiah, the Son of God, who comes into the world" (John 11:27)
- Mary Magdalene, who found the Bridegroom in the garden, clung tightly, and was commissioned to be the first to announce the gospel (John 20:1–18)
- All the women who remained at the cross when the disciples fled, returning to the tomb to find it empty, serving as crucial witnesses to details of the death and resurrection of Jesus Christ (Matt. 27:45–56; Mark 15:40–41; Luke 23:44–49)
- And many more on our way through Scripture to the Revelation bride!

These women all went through the night scenes. But they all gained the vision from the tower and persevered. That's what this text is calling us to.

The interchange between the bride and the Bridegroom helps us to understand our belonging in Christ in the most intimate way. It draws us toward him, encouraging us to stand strong in his eyes and to share this good news with others. It gives us what Richard Bauckham calls freedom in belonging.[59] This belonging arouses us, like the bride, as a fortified holy city, to freely give of ourselves to Christ, the One who gives peace.

---

59. See Richard Bauckham, *God and the Crisis of Freedom: Biblical and Contemporary Perspectives* (Louisville: Westminster John Knox, 2002).

And it evokes us to give and receive in communion with those who come to kiss the Son. By the grace and power of Jesus, may we all collectively stand on that day to see his face.

QUESTIONS FOR DISCUSSION

1. How have you grown spiritually through your own personal night scenes? How has your church grown through trials? How does the greatest commandment, and its Deuteronomic reference, help recalibrate us when we are in night scenes?

2. How do the night scenes in the Song help the church understand our belonging in Christ? How, then, does that belonging inspire us, like the bride, as a fortified holy city, to freely give and receive with those who come to kiss the Son? What can the night scenes teach us about the importance of bringing darkness to light—naming abuse—as well as where our focus is as the bride?

3. Desire has a cost, whether it is rightly or wrongly oriented. How does that factor into your "counting the cost" then in personal life, church life, and family life? Are we willing to make ourselves vulnerable for properly oriented desire? Or do we make sure that vulnerability is carried by someone else? Who pays the cost in different situations? Is it worth it?

Chapter Seven

MALE AND FEMALE VOICE

Radical biblical feminists like to say that the Bible is a patriarchal construction put together by the most powerful men. It's the male voice. Male power. We can't argue with some of this charge—the Bible is androcentric in its authorship. However, given the patriarchal historical context in which it is written, it is quite amazing to look at the female voice in Scripture. It often, as Richard Bauckham notes, interrupts and dominates the male voice, making visible the invisible, telling the story behind the story.[1] Not only is the female voice there, but it sheds light. It teaches. I've already written more extensively on this function of the female voice in Scripture in another book.[2] In this chapter, I would like to look at both the male and female voice in our metanarrative of the Song of Songs and reflect on what the Holy Spirit is saying to the churches today through his Word. There are so many observations, we can merely scratch the surface. But as with the rest of this book, my intention is to make us all singers of the Song, adding our own voices to the chorus.

---

1. Richard Bauckham, *Gospel Women: Studies of the Named Women in the Gospel* (Grand Rapids: Eerdmans, 2002).

2. See Aimee Byrd, *Recovering from Biblical Manhood and Womanhood* (Grand Rapids: Zondervan, 2020).

By talking about voice, I am getting right down to the
nitty-gritty of being human—the crux of dignity and personhood. Diane Langberg lays out three elements to personhood
that abusers often take. She writes of this under the category
of "Power of Personhood."[3] The very first statement she
makes is that "to be human is to have a voice." God created
us as communicators. He spoke the world into existence. He
spoke to Adam and Eve. Today he still communicates with
us through his Word. The gospel is good news that we are to
speak to one another. We speak, we write, and we even sign
with our voices. We can use our voices to communicate love, as
well as indifference and hate. According to Langberg, "Second,
to be human is to be in relationship." We were created for
communion with the triune God and one another—made for
relationship. Isn't that why we have a voice? We were not created to pursue ultimate independence and self-gratification.
We will never find joy and peace in that pursuit. And, "Third,
to be human is to have power and shape the world." Langberg
recognizes the dignity in which God made us when she says,
"Every human life is a force in this world." Power is our agency
to act, to love, to serve, to influence, and to glorify God—or
conversely, to harm, hate, and neglect. Power is our ability to
obey or disobey God. Our power is always derivative, as we are
given it by God and authorized to use it for his glory and our
good. We exercise our power physically, spiritually, intellectually, economically, emotionally, governmentally, verbally,
and more.[4]

So to be human is to have a voice. Our voices are spoken in
relationship. And our voices come with power.

---

3. Diane Langberg, *Redeeming Power: Understanding Authority and Abuse in the Church* (Grand Rapids: Brazos, 2020), 7.
4. Langberg, 4–10.

PLAYFUL VOICES

One of the pleasantries that draws me into the Song is how playful the voices are between the man and the woman. This is interesting to think about, because to speak playfully one must have trust. The lovers have so much familiarity with each other that they can finish one another's sentences. I love the line, right at the end of one of the man's *wasfs*, praising the woman's body from her feet up. As he gets to her face, he says, "Your mouth is like fine wine—" and then the woman completes his sentence, "flowing smoothly for my love, gliding past my lips and teeth!" She then proclaims, "I am my love's, and his desire is for me" (7:9–10). The bride playfully interrupts, entering into his metaphor to respond to his desire, and says that she belongs to him. Here we see what belonging is meant to be— true freedom. Richard Bauckham helps us understand that "the fullest freedom is not to be found in being as free from others as possible, but in the freedom we give to each other when we belong to each other in loving relationships."[5] Belonging is freedom to give, to love. It's "power *to*." The voices in the Song show us the picture of true, uninhibited freedom in belonging exclusively to Christ. This is how we are most fully actualized as human persons.

The woman's voice is so free in the Song. Astonishingly, in its patriarchal context, the female voice is dominant in the Song. A book in the canon of Scripture. Right in the middle. Singing to us. It immodestly begins the Song and closes us out. Female voices make up more than 60 percent of the Song. And yet I'm less interested in the sheer quantity, but in the freedom, boldness, playfulness, intensity, and truth of what the bride

---

5. See Richard Bauckham, *God and the Crisis of Freedom: Biblical and Contemporary Perspectives* (Louisville: Westminster John Knox, 2002), 18.

speaks. She initiates, over and over, starting in the beginning, declaring her desire for the kisses of her Groom's mouth. She needs to get to him, so she asks, "Tell me, you whom I love: Where do you pasture your sheep? Where do you let them rest at noon? Why should I be like one who veils herself beside the flocks of your companions?" (1:7). It's such a bold asking. And he is playful in the beginning of his reply, "If you do not know, most beautiful of women . . ." (1:8). We see this mutual back and forth of compliments and desire, absence and presence.

Mutuality and playfulness are even expressed in how their voices mirror one another. The woman's "for your caresses are more delightful than wine" (Song 1:2) is repeated back to her later by the man: "How delightful your caresses are, my sister, my bride. Your caresses are much better than wine" (4:10). Later, the narrator—Yahweh himself—tells them to "drink, be intoxicated with caresses!" (5:1). The Groom also mirrors the bride, using the phrase "the fragrance of your perfume" (1:3; 4:10). Twice the man says, "Your eyes are doves" (1:15; 4:1) and she mirrors, "His eyes are like doves" (5:12). She waits for him "until the day breaks and the shadows flee," and leading up to their consummation, he reiterates, "Until the day breaks and the shadows flee, I will make my way to the mountain of myrrh and the hill of frankincense" (2:17; 4:6). She picks up on that mountain spiciness at the end of the Song, beckoning, "Run away with me, my love, and be like a gazelle or a young stag on the mountains of spices" (8:14). Also, the woman says that her lover "feeds among the lilies" (2:16; 6:3), and the man describes her breasts "like two fawns, twins of a gazelle, that feed among the lilies" (4:5). What does all this tell us? They are good listeners. They absorb one another's truths. The longing and delights the bride expresses to the Groom are reciprocated. She is beginning to see herself through his eyes. They are united in this one Song, even as they are distinct.

The playfulness, boldness, and dominance of the woman's voice speaks to her freedom in belonging. Freedom comes at a cost. And we know that this belonging cost Christ the most. Jesus modeled this very truth of the cost of freedom for us. He not only did this on the cross but in his whole life on earth. Bauckham mentions one of those examples in Jesus taking on a slave's job of washing feet (John 13:3–15). Jesus loved others by doing something absolutely degrading according to social conventions for a man in his position. In doing so he showed true freedom. "In this act Jesus was free in regarding nothing as beneath him. Whatever others might think, Jesus saw nothing as degrading if he did it for those he loved. In the act of washing feet, he prefigured the shameful, slave's death he was very soon to die. Thus he models the cost of being free for others."[6] We see the fruit of this sung by the voice of the bride in the Song.

BECKONING VOICES

The male and female voices in the Song are beckoning one another and consequently beckoning us. The woman opens the Song wanting kisses and caresses, and beckons, "Take me with you—let's hurry. Oh, that the king would bring me to his chambers" (1:4). She calls him to take her to his inner room behind the veil. That's a big ask right from the start. She sets out straightaway to find him, asking where he is, and he calls her to "follow the tracks of the flock" (1:8). Later he beckons her: "Arise, my darling. Come away, my beautiful one" (2:10). And again (2:13). He calls out, "Let me see your face, let me hear your voice" (2:14). On the day of their wedding, he pleas, "Come with me from Lebanon, my bride; come with me from

---

6. Bauckham, 20.

Lebanon!" (4:8). She responds, summoning the wind! "Awaken, north wind; come, south wind. Blow on my garden, and spread the fragrance of its spices. Let my love come to his garden and eat its choicest fruits" (4:16). The pleas for lovemaking, calling out in absence, and for awaking continue throughout the Song. It ends with the Groom's beckoning, "You who dwell in the gardens, companions are listening for your voice; let me hear you!" And the last line is her response quoted above, calling him to run away with her to the very place her body typifies, the spice-laden mountains of Zion (8:13–14).

In invitations like these, there is both power and vulnerability. There is trust and freedom in initiating. It is a giving of oneself. And yet that is also vulnerable as there is risk of rejection. But we see the confidence dripping in these beckoning calls. We know that there is nothing the Bridegroom has not given. All along he's been calling his bride. She wears this love and is full of anticipation. In receiving this love, she reciprocates. She is encouraged to initiate herself, to ask, to be heard, to give, and to be received in turn. There is constant movement in the Song, as this is a dynamic and fructifying action. The metaphors, imagery, and landscape are enlivened by it, as if the bride is blooming herself, and as we saw earlier, even appropriating marital properties.

Oh, the dynamic power that our voices hold! How inspiring! Isn't it interesting that twice the Bridegroom asks to *hear* the woman's voice? I'd like to look at each case and offer two applications. Calling her his dove, he beckons her out of the clefts of the rock and the crevices of the cliff, saying, "Let me see your face, let me hear your voice; for your voice is sweet, and your face is lovely" (Song 2:14). There is this sense of vulnerability here with the picture of the dove hiding in the crevices for protection. As Christopher Mitchell says, "She must be coaxed and wooed from her place of inaccessibility. . . . The lover must not try forcibly to evict his dove from her hiding place. Only after he gains her trust through his sacrificial love will she emerge and join him."[7] He is sensitive to her. He gives first. He doesn't want her hidden. He not only wants to be there for her, but he wants to see her face. He wants to hear her voice. Why? Because it is sweet and lovely.[8]

I think about this beckoning to his bride both corporately and personally. It's spoken in the context of spring, new life, and restoration. It reminds me of Jeremiah 33:3, in the context of Israel's restoration, where the LORD says, "Call to me and I will answer you and tell you great and incomprehensible things you do not know." What follows is "a sound of joy and gladness, the voice of the groom and the bride, and the voice of those saying, Give thanks to the LORD of Armies, for the LORD is good; his faithful love endures forever as they bring thanksgiving sacrifices to the temple of the LORD" (Jer. 33:11). The Lord reminds his people that his covenant is as sure as his providential ruling of day and night and heaven and earth (33:25).

And what do we hear from the bride in the Song as she responds to this beckoning? She asks him to catch the foxes for them that are trying to ruin the vineyard, as if she is saying, *Make good on your promises, Lord.* She names the foxes, not just because they are trying to destroy her individually, but "for us." And she then takes hold of that covenantal promise, saying, "My love is mine and I am his; he feeds among the lilies" (2:16). Both the asking and the praising are sweet to the Lord. The trust is there. The love is there.

We are personally summoned to call on the Lord in prayer. The Lord wants to hear our voices. We are called to ask him to catch these foxes that are going after the vines of our spiritual

---

7. Christopher W. Mitchell, *The Song of Songs*, Concordia Commentary (St. Louis, MO: Concordia, 2003), 714.

8. And on a broader picture theological note, we see the themes of Israel's exodus from Egypt and the church's exodus from the enslavement of sin playing out in this scene.

and physical lives. And we are called to take hold of his covenantal promise with joy, remembering that he feeds among the lilies. He is with us all along. Don't hide from the Lord. He is calling to hear your voice and see your face. Do we reciprocate his love with our voices? His summons is also a corporate calling to us as the collective bride. She was looking for him, and it turns out she knew where he was all along—among the lilies, with his people. The Lord summons us to gather with his people on the first day of the week to receive Christ and all his blessings through the preached Word and sacrament. Part of that is praying together as a church. How powerful is that voice? He wants to hear it. He calls us to pray to him and promises to answer. But we are not only waiting on his answers; we are seeking his presence. And our voice is sweet to him and our face is lovely. It is a taste of the communion with our Bridegroom and one another that is to come.

The Song ends with another call from the Bridegroom to hear our voice: "You who dwell in the gardens, companions are listening for your voice; let me hear you!" (8:13). Her response is akin to *Maranatha! Come, Lord Jesus!* Our voices are evangelical. We are calling the Lord to Zion, to our mother's house, to the place he is preparing for us. It is an evangelical call, a gospel pronouncement and beckoning to our great telos where we will finally dwell with the Lord in glorified bodies. And it is a call of perseverance to one another to continue to lay hold of Christ, the One who brings us behind the veil. He beckons us to beckon him and one another.

A VOICE THAT JOINS

The voices in the Song tell us something about the symbolic meaning of man and woman. In the beginning of this book,

I proposed that the Song of Songs is a sexual reformation call for the church, analogically enfleshing and revealing the whole metanarrative of Scripture. It sings us into our eschatological hope. The bride's voice is all over the place. As Gregory of Nyssa named her, she is "the teacher"[9] for us who want to sing along.

As I've noted, woman was created second as an eschatological marker. This order is a pattern in Scripture. Meredith Kline discusses this when delineating the "first resurrection" of Revelation 20:5 as a spiritual resurrection, unlike the new heaven and new earth and new Jerusalem in Revelation 21:1–2. He says, "An alternate term for 'new' in Revelation 21 is the word 'second.'"[10] These are two orders—one spiritual, the next bodily and spiritual, indeed "all things" will be made new in the consummation of history, as the second supersedes the first. Kline points out this same language used in Hebrews, talking about the old and new—or second—covenant (cf. 8:7, 8, 13; 9:1, 15, 18; 10:9). And he notes that Paul also used this language when talking about Christ as the second Adam (1 Cor. 15:47).[11] I concur that in this manner, created second, woman represents the second order, arrayed with the glory and radiance of the Son (Rev. 21:11). Her very presence is a beckoning to the telos of mankind.

We first get a picture of the glory realm in the creation story when we read about God's hovering presence (Gen. 1:2). Kline elucidates, "The Glory-Spirit was present at the beginning of creation as a sign of the telos of creation, as the Alpha-archetype of the Omega-Sabbath that was the goal of creation history."[12]

---

9. See Gregory of Nyssa, *Gregory of Nyssa: Homilies on the Song of Songs*, trans. Richard A. Norris Jr., ed. Brian E. Daley and John T. Fitzgerald (Atlanta: Society of Biblical Literature, 2012), 51, and Norris's footnote, "i.e., the Bride, who in Gregory's exegesis of the Song regularly appears in the role of a mistress to her apprentices."

10. Meredith G. Kline, "The First Resurrection," meredithkline.com, https://meredithkline.com/klines-works/articles-and-essays/the-first-resurrection/. Thanks to Anna Anderson for pointing me in this direction.

11. Kline, "First Resurrection."

12. Meredith G. Kline, *Images of the Spirit* (Eugene, OR: Wipf & Stock, 1999), 20.

He also points us to the visible heavens as a testimony to this awaited glory realm that we are to enter.[13] Are we not reminded of this today every time we look up at the sky and contemplate it in wonder? In the creation account, we see that both the Spirit and the woman are testifying to us about this glory realm in creation.

In chapter 3, we saw the significance of the bride joining her voice with the Spirit's, spelled out for us in Revelation 22:17. I've repeated (maybe to the reader's annoyance) this beckoning proclamation call of the bride and the Spirit in that endgame scene to "Come." This is important, as the primary voice we are to be listening for is not the woman's but the Spirit's. This is where the first woman was deceived. And Adam's silence while he was standing there with her magnifies this. Whose voice is doing the calling? Satan's. As Anna Anderson put it, "She listens to Satan who offers her the alien glory of an unholy realm."[14] What a deception! What repercussions! Adam, too, rejected the voice of God, which he heard, and listened to the voice of the woman, who joined with Satan's voice in offering him this alien glory. Anderson continues, "Embedded in her very [body] is the [sign of the] reward of glory extended to him in covenant. Her good work is to help him pass beyond probation and obtain the reward for himself, for her, and all those descending from them by ordinary generation."[15] Instead of helping Adam in their mission to attain this Sabbath-realm, second-order glory, which she typified as woman, she accepted a counterfeit of what her own body represents and therefore failed in her vocation as a necessary ally/helper. Following Satan's voice, she beckoned Adam to come with her, offering him the forbidden fruit. They partook and entered the reign of sin, death, and depravity over mankind.

---

13. Kline, 20.

14. Anna Anderson, "Van Til's Representational Principle Applied to the Woman," Academia, December 16, 2020, 19, https://www.academia.edu/44870840/VAN_TIL_S_REPRESENTATIONAL_PRINCIPLE_APPLIED_TO_THE_WOMAN.

15. Anderson, 19.

In the Song, we see representation restored. The woman's voice is joined with the Spirit's. We see in the first line her desire for the kisses of her Bridegroom's mouth. She speaks her condition to the daughters of Jerusalem: "I am dark like the tents of Kedar, yet lovely like the curtains of Solomon" (1:5). Exploited by her brothers, she hasn't taken care of herself—she is dark from exposure. Yet she is still lovely like the curtains of Solomon. This leads us to think of temple imagery, but there is an echo in this verse that points us right to the glory realm, which both the temple and the heavens represent. In Isaiah we read about God enthroned, "who stretches out the heavens like a curtain" (40:22 NASB). Indeed, he said, "It was my hands that stretched out the heavens" (45:12). Job said, "He alone stretches out the heavens" (Job 9:8). The psalmist also spoke of this testimony in creation, "stretching out heaven like a tent curtain" (Ps. 104:2 NASB). The bride is as lovely as the curtains of heaven, the sign of the Sabbath peace (Solomon) that is to come.[16] The glory Spirit is with her. As Jesus said, "Something greater than Solomon is here" (Matt. 12:42). Woman represents this, which makes her as lovely as the curtains of the glory realm.

The woman, again, beckons us to meditate on the Spirit when she says, "Like an apple tree among the trees of the forest, so is my beloved among the young men. In his shade I took great delight and sat down, and his fruit was sweet to my taste" (Song 2:3 NASB). Teresa of Avila practically sang, "O souls that practice prayer, taste all these words! . . . Oh, what heavenly shade this is!"[17] Her words remind us of the angel's reply to Mary when she was told that she would bear and mother the Son of the Most High: "The Holy Spirit will come upon you, and

---

16. This connection is made in Bernard of Clairvaux, *Sermons on the Song of Songs* (Pickerington, OH: Beloved, 2014), 166.

17. Teresa of Avila, "Meditations on the Song of Songs," in *The Collected Works of St. Teresa of Avila*, vol. 2, trans. Kieran Kavanaugh and Otilio Rodriguez (Washington, DC: ICS, 1980), 248.

the power of the Most High will overshadow you. Therefore, the holy one to be born will be called the Son of God" (Luke 1:35). In light of this future revelation, we have a lot coming together in this verse in the Song. So much to taste! The language of the Spirit's special presence comes together in this shade and overshadowing. The bride's taking great delight in his shade is canonically sandwiched between the "Spirit of God . . . hovering over the surface of the waters" in creation (Gen. 1:2) and this "overshadowing" of Mary's womb.

There are some connections to be made here in light of Richard Whitekettle's work that we looked at in chapter 3, developing this womb/wellspring homology, showing that a woman's body, in its structure and function, corresponds to the order of Levitical sacred space.[18] Did this not culminate in Mary's womb, the sacred space for the dwelling of the Son of the Most High? The woman in the Song uses this language of shade, as if she is sitting under the power of the Most High. Unlike the first woman, who ate the forbidden fruit, she sits "under the shadow of truth."[19] And "the Lord gives from the apple tree"[20] fruit that is sweet to her taste. Eating this fruit from his tree is a sign that she has joined her voice with the Spirit, as later her Bridegroom signifies, telling her that her breath is like apples (Song 7:8, NASB).

Her voice is that of the elect bride of Christ, joined to the Spirit, "the church of the old and new covenant, as well as heaven itself, the Mother of the all-living. Christ, a man, the Seed of the woman, came from heaven to spearhead the heavenward ascent of his bridal people. He came from the glory-realm

---

18. See Richard Whitekettle, "Levitical Thought and the Feminine Reproductive Cycle: Wombs, Wellsprings, and the Primeval World," *VT* 46 (1996): 376–91. He defines homology as "an acknowledged resemblance between two objects based on perceived similarities in structure and function."

19. Teresa of Avila, *Collected Works*, 248.

20. Teresa of Avila, 249.

mother that he might ascend with his glorified bride, forever to partake of consummate joy in fellowship with the Triune God."[21] The man's voice is that of the Bridegroom, the second Adam, the One who is greater than Solomon. Anderson sums it up perfectly that "woman [is] typico-symbolically revealed as the realm of ascent, and man as the means of ascent."[22] And so man is to represent the cruciform headship that our mediator in the covenant of grace established for his bride. It is an order of love in which man is the first to love, the first to sacrifice, and the first to give.

Maybe "glory-realm mother" sounds a bit uncomfortable to you. And maybe you were already uncomfortable with all that Levitical language I referred to above. We see it most typified in the womb of the Virgin Mary. The woman in the Song embraces it. She wants to take her Bridegroom to her mother's house (3:4; 8:2). We don't see any father language in the Song, just mother language—the magic number, seven times (1:6; 3:4, 11; 6:9; 8:1, 2, 5). Anderson is again helpful in following the thread. I must quote her at length:

> At the alpha point of creation in Genesis 1:1, we find the glory realm, the heavens. It is the created sphere of the uncreated Glory-Spirit, the royal house of God which radiates his glory (Is. 66:1, Acts 7:49), which God enters after the work of creation. From this holy realm, God beckons Adam heavenward to pass through probation, to ascend his holy mountain, and to receive in God himself his blessedness and reward (Gen. 2:2–3). This sphere is finally and decisively revealed in feminine terms in Revelation. She is a holy city coming out of heaven from God, as a bride adorned for her

---

21. Anderson, "Van Til's Representational Principle," 23.
22. Anderson, 22.

husband (21:2). And more than like a bride, she is the Bride, the wife of the Lamb, the great, holy mountain city coming out of heaven from God (vv. 9–10). She is both the realm and the people of that realm, his transhistorical church who have overcome and have the right to eat from the tree of life, which is in the paradise of God (2:7). This walled bridal city is the very glory realm of Genesis 1:1, the sphere of Sabbath rest extended in the covenant of works. It is the promise of eternal life—that is, the promise of God himself in a realm beyond Satan and the threat of sin, suffering, and death.[23]

Like the bride of the Song and Revelation, we are to join our voices with the Spirit's, beckoning our "brothers and sisters who hold firmly to the testimony of Jesus" (Rev. 19:10) to "Come!" (Rev. 22:17).

A VOICE THAT BINDS

The voice of the woman, the Shulammite, in the Song, reverberates from the voices of other women in the New Testament. It's quite fascinating how this song gets sung again. Three Marys in the New Testament extend this portrait of woman as mother, sister/friend, and bride.[24] Above we saw a bit of the reverberation of Mary, the mother of Jesus, as a typology of sacred space, the glory realm, the mother's house. Roman Catholics have a history of adding a Marian interpretation to the Song, seeing parallels between the beloved as Israel-church, and Mary as a type of the church as virgin mother.[25]

---

23. Anderson, 17, 18.
24. Thanks to Anna Anderson for making this connection with me.
25. For a commentary faithful to this approach, see Paul J. Griffiths, *Song of Songs* (Grand Rapids: Brazos, 2011).

It is fitting that we see reverberations in the beloved disciple's, John's, gospel. Ann Roberts Winsor wrote a fascinating book on the allusions to the Song of Songs in the fourth gospel.[26] The book begins with a chapter on John 12:1–8, noting the allusions to the Song, including hair, a king reclining, precious nard ointment, feet, and scent, in the account of Mary of Bethany using her hair to anoint Jesus's feet with expensive oil.

We know Mary as the sister of Martha and Lazarus, whom Jesus raised from the dead, and a friend of Jesus. Winsor notes the interpretive difficulty of this text, as commentators try to make sense of why Mary was using her hair for this expressive act. Here was a respectable woman taking down her hair in a room full of men to do something a towel would work much better for. And yet Winsor notes that it made total sense when you realize that John was activating another text here from the Old Testament.[27] While hair is rarely referenced in Scripture, especially in the Old Testament, the Song has five references to it (4:1; 5:11; 6:5; 7:5). The woman's hair is referenced twice in Song 7:5. Here we hear the Groom's voice: "Your head crowns you like Mount Carmel, the hair of your head like purple cloth—a king could be held captive in your tresses." Winsor says, "The unusual mention of the woman's flowing hair in SS 7:[5] and Mary of Bethany's apparently unbound hair in Jn 12:3, in both cases with the king as the object of the hair's 'action,' suggests an allusive link between the texts."[28] Winsor stresses that the wordplay is suggesting that the king is literally bound, or "tied up" by her hair. She takes us to John 18:12 and 18:24, where we see Jesus actually bound when he was arrested.[29]

---

26. Ann Roberts Winsor, *A King Is Bound in the Tresses: Allusions to the Song of Songs in the Fourth Gospel*, Studies in Biblical Literature 6 (New York: Lang, 1999).

27. Winsor, 20.

28. Winsor, 22.

29. Winsor, 22.

John was doing a cover of the Song! And as it was resung, Mary, the sister in Bethany, anointed Jesus for his upcoming burial with her hair. As we see the Song activated, so are all of our senses again. We have this sensual visual of Mary's flowing hair, the touch of it on the feet of the King, the taste of dinnertime at the table, and the smell of expensive perfume filling the house. Do we also not see in Mary the picture of absolute freedom in belonging? She lets down her hair and "washes" his feet. She knows the cost. In the act of anointing his feet with this expensive nard, she prefigures the glory of Christ's death he was very soon to die. She thus models the cost and the fruit of being free for others. "While the king was at his table, my perfume spread its fragrance" (Song 1:12 NIV). And Jesus is captivated by this picture of his sister-bride treasuring him, knowing he will literally become bound for her. He says her hair is like purple cloth, like that of his queen.

A TURNING VOICE

Although I've already spent time on the resurrection scene in John and its connection to the Song, we must return[30] for another look. Winsor points out "bumps in the text"—something that doesn't make plain sense at first glance, therefore making the reader pause and ask why it's there.[31] The second bump was a real treasure for me, after all that work on desire for chapter 4. One of the bumps we've already covered. In John 20:17 Jesus told Mary Magdalene not to cling to him. Winsor notes the oddness of this being said without any prior reference to Mary touching him. What indication do we have for this response?

---

30. Do you see what I did there with the word *return*? Keep reading.
31. Winsor, *A King Is Bound*, 37.

The answer is in the Song, of course, as we've already identified this as an echo from Song 3:4, "I held on to him and would not let him go." But I did not identify the bumps in John 20:14 and 16. In verse 14, Mary "turned around" as she saw Jesus and did not recognize him. But in verse 16, when Jesus called her name, she again was "turning around" as she recognized him and called him *Rabboni*. The repeated word gets the reader's attention, but even more so paints a strange picture. We can picture Mary turning once and facing Jesus. But it is odd that she would turn again when he called her name. It would have to be a complete 360—almost like a dance of joy. It can serve as a conversion moment for the reader.[32]

It certainly was a conversion moment for me, bringing me back to the Song, where we see all kinds of turning. The woman sings, "Until the day breaks and the shadows flee, turn around, my love, and be like a gazelle or a young stag on the divided mountains" (2:17). Later the daughters of Jerusalem ask, "Where has your love gone, most beautiful of women? Which way has he turned? We will seek him with you" (6:1). Also, the Groom says, "Turn your eyes away from me, for they captivate me" (6:5). In Song 6:13, the daughters of Jerusalem sing, "Return, return, O Shulamite; return, return, that we may look upon you" (ESV). And a second party responds,[33] "What would you see in the Shulamite—as it were, the dance of the two camps?" (NKJV). Winsor also points to "Come" in verse 7:11 as a word related to turning. And she says, "It is more than coincidental that the call of the daughters of Jerusalem to the searching woman, 'Turn, turn' should apply so uncannily to Mary Magdalene, the searching woman turning and turning."[34]

---

32. See Winsor, 38.

33. Some commentators say this is the Groom's voice, but there are differing opinions.

34. Winsor, *A King is Bound*, 39.

Earlier I discussed the Greek translation of the woman's desire, the Hebrew *teshuqah*, in Genesis 3:16 as *apostrophē*, signifying the woman's "turning" or "returning" toward her husband. Could this "bump" in the resurrection text be activating more than the Song, even the creation narrative itself? The fulfillment of desire has come to Mary/woman! And so of course she is eager to take him to her mother's house, as the bride in the Song wants to do when she clings to him. She has finally found the one whom her soul loves! Zion is bursting into the garden, but it's not yet time for consummating, as Jesus tells Mary not to cling to him since he hasn't yet ascended to the Father. He has another mission for her, to beckon the disciples as the first herald of the good news (John 20:17). *Let me hear your voice, Mary!* "Companions are listening for your voice," my bride (Song 8:13)!

With these three Marys, we see an emerging portrait of Zion reverberating from the Song: mother of Jesus, sister/friend, and bride. They intertwine in the Song, as each must be evaluated in light of the others. We find ourselves in these voices. Additionally, we are like the nameless woman at the well in John 4—the foreign bride who beckoned the whole town to come and see Jesus. We are the Shulammite who finds peace in his eyes. John was a singer of the Song!

SING WITH ME

"Let me hear your voice," the Bridegroom beckons the bride twice in the Song. Does the church encourage all her people the way Christ encourages his bride? He says, "for your voice is sweet" (2:14), and yet many women in the church today, along with other marginalized people, hear the opposite message. They are silenced. They are hindered from contributing in the theological, creative, intellectual heart of church life. In the

Song, we see mutuality and beautiful reciprocity between the male and the female voice. In fact, the bride's voice is dominant, both opening and closing the Song. What does this tell us about leadership? Leadership brings out the voice of others. It encourages, in the true sense of the word: *giving* courage and support. It gives power *to*, because leadership recognizes personhood and dignity in men and women and sees them as gifts. So leadership invests in and facilitates harmony of the voices of God's people. Leadership says, *Let me hear your voice!* Because that is what love says.

As it opened, the Song closes with an evangelical call. And just as the woman's voice opens the song, she also closes it by beckoning for her Groom, calling him to the spiced mountains that her own body represents. Maranatha. The Song calls us all to Zion, provoking our longing and encouraging our hope. We see the woman's voice functioning this way in other parts of Scripture. Wouldn't we expect that even more so now, especially given the revelation of woman's body being rooted in her typico-symbolic representation of mother-bride Zion? While outwardly the church says it values the woman's voice, its governing principles often shut it out. Unlike laymen's voices, laywomen's voices are often limited in the intellectual/theological circles they can contribute to, whom they can teach, and even their capabilities to speak truth as victims of abuse. Not only that, but many women lament how the men in the church are invested theologically more than women. Too often, both in the church and society, women's voices are suspect. Some of the basic elements of personhood—voice, relationship, and power—are stunted, neglected, ignored, or just plain taken from women.

Disclaimer: What I am about to do is in itself a testimony to the suspicion of the female voice. I want to reassure my readers that I am not aiming to take you to the conclusion that the female voice should dominate over the male's. Not at all. I am not building a case to take power from the men and give it all to the women. That would be missing the point—the *power to* point I made earlier. That would just be causing the same problem in reverse. I don't want to get caught up in the power dynamics between men and women that I bemoaned in chapter 1—who dominates whom. I am more interested in the question, *What does it mean?* Since power is inherent in every human, we must begin with how our power represents God. Oriented this way, we understand that we are to use the power we have to love and serve God by loving and serving others. That's true freedom. Sometimes it's by using our own voices, and often it is by encouraging others to use their voices. It's like a song, and it is dynamic and fructifying. Okay, back to our regularly scheduled program.

There are certain words that I previously was inclined to avoid talking or writing about. One of those words is *power*. I was afraid that by using this word, or by speaking of this concept, I would be associated with radical feminists, liberation theologians, or critical theorists, receiving a label rather than a hearing. But in going through some night scenes and trying to make sense of it all, I found that power is inherent in all of us as human beings made in the image of God, and we should talk about how we use it. Not talking about it helps perpetuate abuse. Ah, *abuse*, another word I previously only used in cases of sexual or physical assault. Not anymore. Abuse occurs when power is used to take from others what is not yours. Abuse takes power and agency from others. It depersonalizes them. Furthermore, I never thought I'd use the word *victim* to talk about myself. And then there is the word *voice*. Women start using this word and they are afraid that they sound whiney. After all, you don't hear men talking about their voice.[35]

---

35. Unless they are ethnic minorities, which share some of these same concerns.

In this practical section of the chapter, I want church leaders to think about whether the culture of their church inhibits the voices of others—whether by gender, ethnicity, class, age, or other marginalizing factors. All of God's people make up the bride of Christ. He wants to hear from us. Do the leaders in your church equip the whole bride for this? Do they listen as much as they speak? Do they give opportunities and encouragement to facilitate diversity among the church's teachers—both formally and informally? What do your Bible studies, Sunday schools, and small groups look like—are they all lecture-based, where congregants are being talked at, or are there opportunities to hear their input and questions in discussion? If so, are diverse voices comfortable and encouraged to participate? Are brothers and sisters invigorated to build up one another in the faith with their voices in daily relationship and life—do they feel the honor and weight of that responsibility of the general office of the believer under the special office of the ministry of the Word? What is the fruit from the preached Word in your church—is it received, worn, reciprocated, and multiplied by its hearers? Is church a habitation of liveliness? In other words, does your church body live according to the reality of its telos?

I also want to talk about abuse as it is connected to taking the voice of others. As someone who has had to speak up as a victim of spiritual abuse, I have found myself in a vulnerable position, confronting church officers about how an outsider sees the church, how a victim is impacted by the decisions and process of the system, and how even justice is perceived. It has been a revealing experience. Sadly, some leaders are just plain abusive—using their own voices of power to name-call, intimidate, shame, silence, and slander. That's darkness that doesn't belong in the house of God. Others reveal their indifference to the dignity and personhood of others by not using their voices to rebuke reviling, harassment, and other abuses. Holocaust survivor Elie Wiesel put it well: "What hurts the victim most is not the cruelty of the oppressor, but the silence of the bystander."[36] Abusers abuse because they can—there is a culture that enables it. Not using your voice when the dignity and personhood of others is affronted is fueling abuse.

Confronting abuse is a vulnerable act. The victim speaks from an exposed position. And if this confrontation is occurring in the church, she is doing this as someone who has respect for the office of ministry and relationship with these people. She is too often setting herself in a position where she will be met with silence, personal expressions of care that contradict collective authoritative actions, disbelief, minimizing, retraumatizing, or even turning the tables to blame the victim. Our goals in confrontation should be greater than the basic justice that needs to be met. I'm writing about this now because my goal is for churches and denominations to get ahead of this abuse, learn about it, train pastors, and provide an avenue for victims to communicate, share their stories, be cared for, and build a healthier, loving culture. Far too many abuse cases have gone public in the last few years. The church needs reform in preventing, recognizing, and dealing with abuse. It starts with valuing the voices of her women.

To grow in love here, leaders need to begin reaching out and hearing how their actions, even for justice, affect victims. How do they treat women who speak truth to them? Is that a gift? Or is it a threat? I have done a lot of reflecting about how I want to use my voice as a victim, and how vulnerable and hard that is, while encouraging others to do the same. But the whole reason I have found myself in this nighttime scene is because I tried to use my voice theologically to help the church. I was branded as dangerous. Certainly, churches need to be vigilant in guarding

---

36. Quoted in Carol Rittner and Sondra Meyers, *Courage to Care: Rescuers of Jews during the Holocaust* (New York: NYU Press, 1986), 2.

orthodoxy. We have our confessions of the faith that help us here. I am not saying that every opinion and teaching has equal validity. There is a difference between critique and suppression or abuse. Not critiquing errant teaching is also a sign of devaluing a voice. But how do we treat those with whom we disagree within the bounds of our confessions? Do we have nothing to learn from others? Have we lost our singing voices?

And yet we still sing, because our voices and the power behind them represent our God. Not only that, but he hears them. He calls for our voices. That's why we begin with prayer to the One who gave us a voice and wants us to know of his presence with us. What if we begin by responding to Jeremiah 33:3 and really believing it: "Call to me and I will answer you and tell you great and incomprehensible things you do not know"?

QUESTIONS FOR DISCUSSION

1. In what ways is the woman's voice dominant in the Song of Songs?
2. What are some possible signs to discern whether your voice is joining with the Spirit and the realm of glory, or with Satan and an alien glory of an unholy realm?
3. I ask many questions in the "Sing with Me" portion of this chapter. Go back and reflect on some of these. It would be good for church officers and congregants to discuss some of these together.

Outro

ESCHATOLOGICAL IMAGINATION[1]

The Song of Songs is filled with humanly incomprehensible things that we need to know. Things that we could never imagine on our own. Things that we need the new life of the Spirit to begin to understand. Returning to John Lennon's hit song "Imagine" after singing the Song of Songs reveals the *lack* of imagination in his lyrics. Sadly, many Christians read Scripture with no imagination—like there are no heavenly realities concretely working through the text in our lives today. They read with modern metaphysical and critical methods, believing they are being faithful to the plain sense of the text. We surely do not want to incorporate meaning into the authoritative text of Scripture that is not there, but our good intentions have not taken into account the providence of God in divine authorship.[2] To read the Song of Songs this way is to read it as if there is no heaven. It is to read it as if it is not in the canon of Scripture.

Now that we've tasted the new wine, we can't go back. We've seen that intertextual quotes, allusions, and echoes pointing us to the eschatological metanarrative in God's Word

---

1. I borrowed this title from Trevor Hart, "Eschatological Imagination," *Transpositions: Theology, Imagination and the Arts* (blog), April 29, 2011, http://www.transpositions.co.uk/eschatological-imagination/.

2. See Hans Boersma, *Scripture as Real Presence: Sacramental Exegesis in the Early Church* (Grand Rapids: Baker Academic, 2017).

are discovered gifts from the divine Author, not impositions or mere speculations. They make up the precious jewels inlaid in our nuptial gown.

In the introduction, I asked you to imagine heaven and earth coming together. Well, it has! And the typology of man and woman has been telling this story all along. The whole Old Testament is building up our longing and pointing to this truth. In Jesus Christ, heaven meets earth. As fourth-century bishop Athanasius of Alexandria put it, "The self-revealing of the Word is in every dimension—above, in creation; below, in the Incarnation; in the depth, in Hades; in breadth, throughout the world. All things have been filled with the knowledge of God."[3]

Imagine reading Scripture and living our lives with these eyes. This is what Jesus told his disciples to do as he revealed this hermeneutic to them on the road to Emmaus. But even though their hearts were burning, he still had to give them the eyes to see. He did it through the Word proclaimed, hospitality and fellowship at the table, and the sacrament of bread and wine. He beckoned all of their senses as he revealed himself, present with them. He does the same with all of his beloved disciples. We gather together to receive Christ and all his blessings at the beginning of each week, heaven and earth coming together, the future interrupting the present.

Like the disciples on the road to Emmaus, we can have the Word of Christ and yet miss the Word himself. As a result, we can't properly articulate our desires and understand our own sufferings. We chase after counterfeit lovers. We devalue life. We stereotype our sexuality. Our ideologies cannot give us the peace we seek. Then we come to the Song, and it summons our deepest desires within us. It weaves together all the tapestry of the history of God's people, the words of the prophets, and the

---

3. Athanasius of Alexandria, *On the Incarnation*, trans. Penelope Lawson (n.p., England: Pantianos Classics, 1944), 32.

wisdom writings, revealing what we were created for and there-fore the picture of ultimate blessedness. We see that we long for the beatific vision—to behold the face of the Bridegroom. The Song enacts retrieval like the last runner in a relay—taking the baton that has been passed by her teammates, while running with her eyes on the finish line, to Jesus. He is the blessing. He is our end. The Song is apocalyptic in this way—it lifts the veil. We have the whole metanarrative in concentrate. Our senses are aroused, and our imaginations are activated. With a swig of this new wine, we see how reductive and earthly our views about ourselves and others are, even in the church. Our own stories are exposed as narrow and hollow.

Our limitedness as creatures prevents us from comprehend-ing it fully. How can we ever exhaustively know the love of God for his people? But we can begin to see. And we are thirsty. The Song is in the canon of God's Word because he wants to reveal himself to us and he delights in his people. It's not to be read empirically as some sort of manual about virginity and mar-riage. The Song explains spiritual things for spiritual people (1 Cor. 2:13). And it is enfleshed in man and woman, with all of nature joining in. Then all the other matters fall into place. In Jesus Christ, heaven and earth come together—he leaves his "mother's house," the heavenly realm, to cling to his bride and usher her into his inner chambers (Gen. 2:24).

UNITING OUR TWO WORLDS

The Song of Songs unites our two worlds, the visible and the invisible. And it ignites our eschatological imagination. If, as John Lennon suggests, we imagine no heaven, then we lose our imaginations—we lose our ability to see all the treasures and see how they belong on the dress. Trevor Hart explains:

In matters of eschatology, as elsewhere, God makes himself and his purposes and promises known not by downloading a body of digitised factual data, but by taking our imaginations captive, lifting us up through Spirit-filled reading to "see" and "taste" the substance of things lying way beyond our proper purview and calling us in turn responsibly to imagine further, allowing our extrapolations and ornamentations (which duly take a dynamic "lived" form) to be guided and tested by the trajectories of divinely furnished prototypes. The trajectories along which Christian eschatological imagining travels are indeed set securely in Scripture itself, which encourages it to extrapolate both positively and negatively from features of life in the here-and-now.[4]

It is the heavenly realities that inform the way we understand the world. These truths provoke wonder, gratitude, and imagination to live in light of their certainty. We participate in this eschatological imagination together as a church. And we have the liturgy of corporate worship that recalibrates us to this trajectory.

What does this all have to do with the sexual reformation? Can't you see it? Our bodies are not merely biological. We know this intuitively. It is why sexual abuse is so traumatic—it is a deep violation of personhood and our eternal value. Our bodies are not merely earthly. They are part of the trajectories of divinely furnished prototypes! We have souls that are united to our bodies. Something both visible and invisible is represented in our beings. Our bodies are theological. And we are to be theologians, knowing the true God who created us. As Timothy Tennent says, "To put it simply, a theology of the body means that we understand the body as not merely a biological

---

4. Hart, "Eschatological Imagination."

category but supremely as a theological category, designed for God's revelatory and saving purposes."[5] This opens up our imaginations to behold the glory of God and the glory in which he made man and woman.

Despite the saying, focusing on heavenly realities and our true telos does a *lot* of earthly good. It orients our desires from, through, and back to Christ (Rom. 11:36). We read his Word better, as it isn't just examining a text through empirical methods but searching for his presence in it. We realize that understanding is a gift of his Spirit. We view our own bodies differently, as they are meant to house the Holy Spirit. We look at one another differently, as whole persons with whom we are to enjoy communion with the triune God together. We take sin seriously, and under the reign of grace repent, turning our eyes toward Christ. We want to use our minds and bodies to serve him and one another. We exercise empathy because we understand the effects of the fall and suffering before glory. We "speak and act as those who are to be judged by the law of freedom" (James 2:12). We share God's Word with more expectation. We take seriously the great honor and responsibility to proclaim God's Word to one another, which Derek Taylor explains is "what happens when God's Word in Scripture becomes concrete here and now."[6] It *gives* Christ. And therefore it transforms our ethics.

The man, in his typology, shows us that this transformation is based on the love of the second Adam, expressed in sacrificial giving. The woman, in her typology, directs our focus heavenward. She sets us in motion. And this is what the bride in the Song does.

---

5. Timothy C. Tennent, *For the Body: Recovering a Theology of Gender, Sexuality, and the Human Body* (Grand Rapids: Zondervan Reflective, 2020), 14.

6. Derek W. Taylor, *Reading Scripture as the Church: Dietrich Bonhoeffer's Hermeneutic of Discipleship* (Downers Grove: IVP Academic, 2020), 178.

How do we bring this heavenly reality into our lives now? We can start by recognizing that both men and women need agency. Both sexes are potent. Both are benevolent. Both are gifts. Both are already whole in Christ. The way we relate is based on the love of Christ, our Bridegroom, our Elder Brother, our Friend. So-called mature masculinity recognizes the need for women's contribution in more than the domestic realm (in which men, too, serve domestically). Both male and female voices participate in eschatological imagination, which includes diverse ways of contributing formally and informally as disciples participate in the theological life of the church. Our typologies are descriptive, telling the story of the spousal love of God. While they direct us, they are not rigidly prescriptive—hence, our earlier example that although woman in her typology represents the peace of the second order, Deborah (and Jael) were not sinning as allies in war. Likewise, with the woman who bravely intervened to negotiate with Joab while he was leading a siege on her city. She convinced him that he didn't want to "destroy a city that is like a mother in Israel" (2 Sam. 20:19). She then counseled the people of her city to seek out the rebellious Sheba, cut off his head, and throw it over the city wall. She was called wise (2 Sam. 20:16). She was not accused of "trying to usurp male authority." How's that for showing reciprocity?

The trajectories of our relationships fit into our typico-symbolic representation as man and woman. Women are daughters, sisters, aunts, wives, and mothers. Men are sons, brothers, uncles, husbands, and fathers. Single, chaste lives point to that longing for the coming of our Bridegroom, while representing that they are whole persons in him, not in another, not in a role they perform. Singles also represent that one relational attribute toward one another that extends into eternity: sisters and brothers.

Married couples picture the exclusive covenant love of Christ and his bride. This is why we uphold marriage between one man and one woman, as I said before. Sexual distinction is meaningful in one-flesh union. It demarcates these other distinctions: creator/creature, earth/heaven, visible/invisible. And yet we don't just marry any person of the other sex. Those who marry find particular meaningfulness in that person they chose for a spouse, as an unrepeatable person in whom they delight. Likewise, God's electing love for his people is not arbitrary.[7] This point also brings value to our friendships, work, and ministry partners. Our bodies, our whole personhoods, are gifts bestowed with dignity by God. This is why we promote holiness in one another in all of our relationships.

And our typology even speaks to the issue of the valuation of prenatal life. The womb represents fullness of life, the inner sanctum of the divine realm. In the act of giving birth, woman typifies the birth of the church through messianic suffering. The womb is a prototype of that true, fortified city. A mother's cries in labor are proleptic of Christ's on the cross—signifying the emergence of the church from the womb of the dawn (Ps. 110:3). Does this not render the question of when life begins superfluous? When a woman misses a menstruation, her "waters are bounded" in a sense, to nurture life, and not to flow again until birth. Do we not see in this the valuation of Christ for his people, who, born of a woman, took on human life so that the heavens would birth the church through the agony of the Son from heaven?[8] We are called to this valuation of life! We are called even to sacrifice our own bodies to nurture it. We are called to trust in the invisible inner workings of God in our wombs, "the place of God's originating . . . life the secret workplace of the

---

7. It's not based on any good he sees in us, but out of his "great love that he had for us" (Eph. 2:4).

8. Thanks to Anna Anderson for contributing to my thoughts here.

Almighty."[9] Additionally, the metaphysical understanding of the unity of our souls and bodies adds to the value of unborn babies. Scripture doesn't tell us at what point in a pregnancy the baby's body and soul unite, because the separation of our bodies and souls means death. And we know that when we die, our souls are with the Lord. And yet our bodies still groan with the earth, waiting for that great day when our Bridegroom will come for us, ushering in the new heavens and the new earth; glorifying our new bodies, reunited with our souls; singing the eschatological nuptials preluded in the Song of Songs.

RESTORING THE DIGNITY AND PERSONHOOD OF MAN AND WOMAN

Sexual reformation in the church is not primarily about man or woman. We are reforming our very understanding of who the triune God is and the end of his works in creation. Man and woman are made in the image of God; therefore God must be the ultimate end for our sexuality. Before discussing the love of God for his people and his works outside himself, we have, as Scott Swain describes, "something inside God himself, namely the three persons of the Trinity and their eternal, mutual life of knowledge and love."[10] In the introduction, I said that I hoped the biggest takeaway for the reader is the awe of beholding our God. That is our end. As Swain explains,

> Our salvation is finally ordered to Jesus, God's beloved Son, the supreme good eternally loved by the Father in the Spirit,

---

9. Leland Ryken, James C. Wilhoit, Tremper Longman III, eds., *Dictionary of Biblical Imagery* (Downers Grove, IL: IVP Academic, 1998), 962.

10. Scott R. Swain, *The Trinity: An Introduction*, Short Studies in Systematic Theology (Wheaton, IL: Crossway, 2020), 124.

the final end appointed by the Father in the Spirit in his eternal decree, the final end toward which the Father in the Spirit moves all things in his providence. All of God's external works and the new creation itself are a theater for his glory, "that in everything he might be preeminent (Col. 1:18), "to the glory of God the Father" (Phil. 2:11).[11]

The triune God is a personal God who is in personal, perfect fellowship with himself. He does not need or benefit from communion with us, and yet he made us alive in Christ "because of his great love that he had for us" (Eph. 2:4). His love overflows out of who he is. Swain continues,

> God—who, in eternity, crowns his beloved Son in the Spirit—creates, redeems, and consummates the world in order that he might, in time, crown his beloved Son in the Spirit, installing him as "the highest of the kings of the earth" (Ps. 89:27), the heir of the nations (Ps. 2:8); the head of the body (Eph. 1:22–23); and the husband of the bride (Eph. 5:32): "the most handsome of the sons of men" (Ps. 45:2), the loveliest, most desirable, most satisfying object of all loves, desires, or satisfactions. There is no greater good, there is no higher end.[12]

This is why Jesus prayed for us to see his glory (John 17:24–26). It is our greatest good! I've noted that he prayed as if he were already in heaven, longing for that great day of coronation and consummation when the Father will crown him, and that his bride is the crown with which he will be crowned. How wondrous to imagine! Jesus was praying for us to know the Father, for in this knowing we will love the Son as the

---

11. Swain, 125.
12. Swain, 126.

Father does, and he will dwell within us. It's worth repeating Kelly Kapic again here: "In Jesus, God actualizes his call to us to enter communion with him through the Son and by the Spirit."[13] We are persons made for personal communion with a personal God. Swain reminds us that "in this the Father is glorified; in this the fruit of the Spirit is exhibited; in this our joy is made full (John 15:8, 11)."[14]

Our telos epitomizes our dignity and personhood. God loves each and every one of his people. So, just as we cannot flat-foot the Song as a horizontal love-and-sex manual, we cannot flat-foot our sexuality under the weight of cultural conventions. The church has incorporated an Aristotelian anthropology with an unmoored pietism that misses what Pope John Paul II called the very "glory of the human body before God" and the "glory of God in the human body, through which masculinity and femininity are manifested."[15] It misses both our dignity and personhood as unique human beings created in the image of the triune God for personal communion with him and one another. As Anna Anderson says, "We are diverse and cannot be reduced to a list of abstractions." Men and women are not abstract categories, but persons. "Those abstractions enslave, but our sexuality viewed eschatologically frees us to run forward in freedom, not fall under the weight of cultural mores."[16] She adds that we cannot have both this classical Christian piety based on sex polarity and the integral complementarity that understands that our sexuality is anchored in eschatology. One is an approach from below and the other an approach from above. The latter emphasizes the archetypes in

---

13. See Kelly Kapic, "Anthropology," in *Christian Dogmatics: Reformed Theology for the Church Catholic*, ed. Michael Allen and Scott R. Swain (Grand Rapids: Baker Academic, 2016), 167.

14. Swain, *Trinity*, 126.

15. See John Paul II, *Man and Woman*, TOB 57:3, 353.

16. Anna Anderson, personal communication.

light of the metanarrative by God's grace to compel it forward. "One leads to shame and the other leads to glory."[17]

And that is where sexual reformation begins, by looking forward to the glory of the triune God, sharing in the Father's love for the Son by the Spirit. That is how we image God. That is where we find not only peace but true delight. Our sexuality signifies the gift of the Father's love for the Son in giving him a bride. And this delineates the spousal love of God for his people.

ESCHATOLOGICAL BLESSING

We long to be blessed by God, to be kept by the Lord to the end, to behold him, so that his face makes our own shine with his radiance as it's turned toward his bride, and we can join with the Father in loving the Son by the Spirit.

The psalms of ascent echo our eschatological hope and spark our eschatological imagination. Psalm 121 highlights Christ as our keeper. It opens with our hope: "I lift my eyes toward the mountains" (v. 1). Zion is immediately in the picture. E. W. Hengstenberg explains that this psalm is to be read in conjunction with Psalm 122. They are both likely pilgrim songs sung at the end of their journey, on that last-night watch, before lying down for rest from all their traveling. Psalm 121 was sung when the sojourners could see the mountains of Jerusalem in the distance. He writes that Psalm 122 would be sung at the next station, when they made it to the city gates. They would sing it "when the sacred pilgrim trains had reached the gates of Jerusalem, and halted for the purpose of forming in order, for the solemn procession into the Sanctuary . . . Psalm 134." What do we see in Psalm 134? As the call to evening worship ends,

---

17. Anna Anderson, personal communication.

we see a benediction: "May the LORD, maker of heaven and earth, bless you from Zion" (v. 3). That's what we long for.

Jesus Christ "keeps" us on our pilgrimage to our eschatological blessing. We can rest in him. In Psalm 121 we see the LORD as the keeper for Israel, saying, "'I keep thee,' which was addressed to the patriarch as he slept on his pilgrimage: and this also 'he neither slumbereth or sleepeth' is seen in its true light."[18] These psalms are echoed in the Song. There are the reverberations of gate, shade, Zion, mountain, sun smiting by day, night, peace, prosperity, love, walls, and the LORD blessing us from Zion.[19] In the creation account, we read that God put the man in the garden to cultivate it and to keep it (Gen. 2:15). Adam let evil in the gate, into the sacred space—he slumbered. He was the neglectful gatekeeper, or guardian, of the walls. Was Satan trying to obtain the blessing, ascending the mountain on his own? He deceived the woman into losing sight of who she was and of her vocation as an ally to Adam in their mission toward that eschatological blessing. There was no blessing in taking what was not theirs, but curse. Satan was made as low to the ground as could be, immediately.[20] He will not ascend. But he cannot have God's people. Jesus, the second Adam, ushers his bride to the mountain.

Perhaps the author of the Song had these pilgrim songs in mind, approaching the gate of Jerusalem at the end of their

18. E. W. Hengstenberg in Charles Spurgeon, *The Treasury of David*, vol. 3 (pt. 2) (1869; repr., Peabody, MA: Hendrickson, 1988), 17.

19. *Gate:* Ps. 122:2; Song 7:4,13; *Shade:* Ps. 121:5; Song 2:3; *Zion:* Ps. 134:3; Song 3:11; *Mountain:* Ps. 121:1; Song 2:17; 4:6, 8; 8:14; *Sun Smiting:* Ps. 121:6; Song 1:6; *Night:* Ps. 121:6; 134:1; Song 3:1; 5:2; *Peace:* Ps. 122:7, 8; Song 8:10; *Prosperity:* Ps. 122:9; Song 8:12; *Walls:* Ps. 122:7; Song 8:9, 10; *Blessings from Zion:* Ps. 134:3; Song 5:1b; *Love:* Ps. 122:6; Song 1:16; 2:4, 5, 10, 16, 17; 3:1, 2, 3, 4, 5, 10; 4:16; 5:2, 4, 5, 6, 8, 9, 10, 16; 6:1, 2, 3, 4; 7:6, 9, 10, 11, 13; 8:4, 6, 7, 14.

20. See Valerie Hobbs, *High Places: A Meditation on Jesus's Healing in Mark 2:1–12,* Lamp of the Lamb, February 4, 2021, https://www.youtube.com/watch?fbclid=IwA R04p4kSoYfQxVGyo54gCEOgCtHlYO7QBrqm2AlZ59lwl3ZgT3oHvum9ojU&v=4 1lu-IhBmmE&feature=youtu.be.

journey to the sanctuary, wanting to receive this blessing from the Lord. But the Song goes further than these psalms. The bride begins by asking for the kisses of his mouth, to be taken to his chambers, and to know where he lets his sheep rest at noon. She takes us right to the eschatological blessing. His caresses are better than wine. She takes us to the divine embrace. And in the Song we have the prosopological blessing from the Father, speaking to the Son and the bride at their wedding consummation, "Eat, friends! Drink, be intoxicated with caresses!" (5:1). This is the day for which we long!

Until then we have the lyrics. We can have a taste of the holy of holies in the heart of God's Word, full of incomprehensible things that we need to know. Until then we sing,

> Run away with me, my love,
> and be like a gazelle
> or a young stag
> on the mountains of spices. *(Song 8:14)*

Maranatha! Come, Lord Jesus!